DEATH
AND OTHER DANCES

Carla Harvey

To Contact the Author:
www.carlaharvey.com

ISBN-13: 978-0-9960137-0-3
ISBN-10: 0-99601-370-9

First Edition – 2014

Cover Design by Johnny Jones for C.O.M.A.
www.creativeonlinemusicart.com

Interior Layout by Gianna Carini
www.brighteyes.org

Author Bio Image (on back cover)
Photographer: Laura DeSantis-Olsson

DEATH
AND OTHER DANCES

Carla Harvey

Pretty Girls Do Ugly Things Publishing

For my husband and my father

CONTENTS

1.

WE'RE ALL TERMINAL

THE FIRST TIME I SAW SOMETHING DIE, I was four years old, sitting in the backseat of my grandmother's Buick. Usually I was fixated on the hole that had rusted through the floorboards of her car, exposing the world speeding beneath my feet; but on that day I stared out the backseat window. Across the median, a dog was loose in the mid-afternoon traffic. We stopped at a light just as a car struck the black Lab, grinding its paw into the pavement. The dog desperately tried to lift his foot, confused as to what had made it so suddenly and irreversibly immobile. He struggled and gnawed at the street as the light changed from red to green. Just when I thought he might free himself, another car struck him and his body lay motionless, red fluid spilling from it.

I thought about the dog for days. I began to notice that death was all around me. Birds hit my window, fell down, and lay still in the grass. A neighborhood cat also met its fate against the tire of an oncoming pile of American steel and it stiffened, tongue forever protruding out, just two doors down. Even my hamsters could only be kept alive for a month or so before I'd find them curled into a furry fetal position with excrement creeping out of their behinds. The crimson vines that splayed from the black Lab's midsection came back to me repeatedly in my sleep.

I wanted to see it again.

I smashed bugs with my feet but it wasn't the same. I longed to see what was inside the rabbits in my backyard, to sneak attack them with a rock, to see the life leave their little bodies. When my grandfather died a few months later, I felt very strongly that my sudden morbid fascination must have in some way caused his demise.

Granddaddy was a light-skinned black man with dark freckles, a hint of Cherokee blood, and a sideways gait, who drank himself to death just after his 50th birthday.

"Come give me some sugar, sugar dumpy lumpy," he would say, and I would run into his thin, outstretched arms. His lips were always wet. I loved him desperately. The last time I saw him alive, he was a grey body stretched out in a hospital bed with an oxygen mask on.

One evening, my mother and father sat my brother and I down in my room.

"Granddaddy had to go to heaven today," my mother said, stroking my hair. My father stared at the wall. My yellow curtains and Holly Hobby bedspread were too bright for my parent's somber mood. We looked at them blankly, knowing something terrible had occurred, but not quite sure how to react. The Italian in my mother had made her God-fearing and a firm believer in a happier place, but at three and four years of age, heaven meant nothing to us, and even less to my stone-faced father.

There were viewings that week for my Granddaddy but I didn't want to go. On the second day, my mother put me in tights and a dress and made me. It was snowing, and everyone I'd ever known in my short life met in a parking lot and marched up the icy sidewalk to the church. There was my Uncle Glen, whom I hadn't forgiven for calling me "Bucky Beaver" as I'd eaten an ice-cream cone that summer, Uncle Dorsey and his wild mop of hair, Great Uncle Kenneth and his spotted half-fingers that had been sliced in a factory, and my father's sister, Denise, who was the prettiest girl I'd ever seen.

Inside the church, my Grandmother Renata, who we weren't allowed to call "Grandmother" because she felt she looked too young for such an ominous title, sat with her head high, the collar of her fur coat enveloping her like a Queen's ruff. She had divorced Granddaddy nearly a decade before; the man on display in front of us was a far cry from the handsome Korean War veteran she'd married and made four children with. She looked on with indifference as Tommy, Granddaddy's portly, ebony girlfriend, clung to his casket, quaking with grief until she was escorted away so that the rest of us could have a look.

After a short service, everyone lined up to say their final goodbyes to Walter Franklin the First.

When it was my turn, I went to the casket with my father, Walter Franklin the Second. He lifted me up so that I could see my Granddaddy, dressed in a new suit, shoes shined. The pungent smell of floral arrangements hung in the air, overwhelming me. Heaven? I didn't believe it! How could Granddaddy be in heaven when he was right here and I could touch him? I knew my mother was feeding me stories. Granddaddy was just dead, dead as the black Lab on Woodward Avenue.

2.

SOMEWHERE BETWEEN CINDERELLA
AND THE BIBLE

Highland Park, California, 2012

"THIS ONE IS COMPLETELY REMODELED, with three bedrooms and two baths." A weary real estate agent fumbled with a lock box, finally procuring two keys. "The area is up-and-coming," he lifted his eyebrow at an old Mexican man stumbling down the street and shifted his stance to shield our view from the undesirables of the neighborhood. He needed to make this sale. Times were hard. His wife was on his ass.

I stood on the front steps of a duplex in Highland Park with a 41-year-old man named Anthony Allen. I clutched his hand as we walked through the front room. The duplex had an open floor plan and sunlight beamed through the window. There was a sizable kitchen with polished granite countertops and shiny appliances. *Maybe I'll learn to cook*, I thought to myself. There was even a converted workspace so that Anthony could run his luthier business from home. Domestic bliss beamed at us from every corner of the house.

"Do you like it?" I asked, and looked up at him.

He smiled back at me and pushed the hair out of my eyes. I pushed it back.

I fell in love with Anthony Allen before I knew a thing about him. I was performing at a dive bar on Santa Monica Boulevard, electrical tape swathing my brown nipples, covered in blood and screeching out the Misfits' "Where Eagles Dare" the first time I saw him. He stood out in the crowd in his black leather jacket, as much James Woods as he was Sid Vicious. *Not my usual type*, I thought to myself as I shimmied my way closer to him, but I was intrigued nonetheless.

After my set, I caught him in the doorway to the smoking patio.

"I like you," I said, poking him in the stomach.

He gave me wry smile and I ran away like a tongue-tied schoolgirl. I was smitten before hearing the sound of his voice. For all of my blood-and-beer-spitting bravado, I couldn't speak to the man.

The idea of "love at first sight" had always been a frivolous one to me. My mother said she'd known she would marry my father from the first time she saw him across the room at a crowded party. But she'd been an impressionable 18-year-old girl at their meeting, and I was a woman who didn't have the time to be swayed by novel ideas or romantic notions.

By the time I met Anthony, I'd already been through the wringer; I'd been dragged across front lawns by my ankles, I'd dug deep into the carpet for crumbs of cocaine at five in the morning on a Tuesday—I'd even cleaned the shit out of a corpse's ass. Truth had already cemented itself in my heart: People were liars and cheaters, and love was a fallacy, best shelved alongside *Cinderella*, the Bible, and the Polaroid of my pregnant mother and father in front of Detroit City Hall after their shotgun wedding.

People often spoke of this Anthony Allen like he was a mythical creature. Everybody had something good to say. I'd heard he was the best luthier in town, he played bass like a motherfucker, and that he was a loyal, upstanding guy. I didn't actually get introduced to him until he showed up backstage at the House of Blues one night to play a gig with a misanthrope I'd been seeing, *and it was him*, the man in the leather jacket who had left me speechless at my show.

That night, when he walked into the dressing room area, every hair on both my arms raised. I felt like a cretin underneath his cool, blue gaze. I mean, he was Anthony Allen! And I... Well, I was just a silly girl that bounced around with electrical tape on her nipples singing punk rock songs.

I slithered across the backstage couch, folding my arms on top of a brocade pillow. The air was thick with voodoo like it always was in those hallowed rooms where the greats had relaxed before their shows.

"I hear you're from Michigan, too," I said. *Stupid*, I thought. *Now he would know that I'd asked about him.*

"Yes! Kalamazoo." He smiled back at me and I

knew he recognized me. He sat down on the couch next to me, crossing his legs. His jeans were tight, and my stare wandered down to his crotch before making way back to his eyes. I felt at ease sitting there next to him. I imagined that in some parallel universe where we were already comfortable, he would've reached out to stroke my hair or my hands, his touch soft yet deliberate. It would be perfect. I smiled at the thought of it, blushed, and looked down at the brocade pillow in my lap.

After the misanthrope and I parted ways, I was happily single for a while and enjoying the solitude. I'd relaxed into just being *me*. But suddenly, I found myself thinking about this Anthony. I'd never deliberately pursued a man before. I let them come to me.

But, goddamn, I really wanted this one.

I had no idea what his reaction would be if I contacted him. In an attempt at a passive play, I invited him to a see my band perform on a Saturday night. When he showed up in a long leather coat and offered to help me carry the sawed-off torso I was using as a stage prop into the club, I was besotted.

From that night on, we were inseparable. And now, we were house-shopping.

"I do like this house," he said, smiling back at me. "I can finally keep all of my gear at home, and this kitchen is amazing."

I searched his face for signs of pressure or stress. He was, after all, a 41-year-old unmarried man that I had just begun to date a year ago. Maybe he didn't want all of this. Maybe he didn't really want me.

My palms were sweating in his big hands as we walked through the bedrooms—a master and a second.

"Are you two planning on having children? Mount Washington Elementary is one of the best in the nation; they focus on the arts."

I was getting dizzy. *Children?* I had a brief vision of my belly stretched by a set of twins, ironing, cooking, and cleaning while Anthony was out banging whores on tour. Our savings accounts would be fused, our lives intertwined, completely attached. And attachment... Well, attachment could only lead to disappointment, right? Need would most certainly make me weak.

I have this thing with people: I look at them and all I can think about is how much it'll hurt when they're gone. On a dinner date with someone new, I'll plan their funeral by the main course. I bury them before dessert. I've moved on by the time the check arrives.

I ran outside for air, planting myself on the front steps of the duplex, head in my hands.

3.

BORN IN A CITY BUILT TO RUST
Southfield, Michigan, 1980's

I CROUCHED IN THE SHADOWS OF OUR LIVing room, ginger brown curls in front of my eyes. At five years old, I assessed my situation; there was no telling which direction the danger would come from. I wedged myself between a wood paneled wall and my father's prized, plastic-covered velvet couch. Sunlight streamed through the windows, catching thick rays of dust that danced around me and tickled my nose. I controlled my breathing so that I wouldn't shake the branches of the white acrylic tree next to me. I was still. Focused. Listening.

Then I was off, darting across the room, determined. I'd almost made it to the last wooden beam of the ranch house when I felt it—my legs buckled and I tried to pull myself forward but my body had become immobile. I was caught. My mother's hands grasped my ankles, dragging me backwards as I clutched at the carpet. I threw my head back to look at her and she growled at me through her hair, long and parted down the middle. My brother, one year younger than me yet always my savior, jumped on her back from behind and she released my legs, laughing her big beautiful laugh. Tears rolled down her cheeks. Mad Dog was our second favorite game.

Our absolute favorite game was the one we'd play in my mother's red Escort. We'd drive to the market with her, and right around Telegraph Road, a pained expression would darken her olive face.

"What, Mama?" My heart would race as the other Fords and Chevrolets sped by us. "Mama! What!"

"I can't move my arm! I think it's broken!" she'd exclaim, her brow furrowed. She was a convincing actress. She could've been one, really. "You kids have to do the stick shift." She lifted her hands off the wheel, shaking them limply.

"No!" my brother would cry. We couldn't do it! How *could* we do it?

When our pleas escalated to a pitch that annoyed her enough, she would put her hands back on the wheel and laugh at us.

My father was rarely around for these games. He worked the midnight shift at the Rouge Steel Plant for Ford Motor Company. In those days, it seemed that all the fathers in the area worked for Ford, GM, or Chrysler. When he got home from his shift, he would sleep and we'd tiptoe around until he was ready to see us. When my mom got a job in an optical shop, my father's sleep pattern was interrupted. He had to get up and fix us our lunch. It was always the same: boiled kielbasa on Wonder bread, topped with a thin line of cheap mustard and served up hot while we watched *Woody Woodpecker*. Then he would shuffle back to bed. Sometimes, I would curl up in the hallway and listen to him snore.

In the late seventies and eighties the autoworkers in Detroit were kings. The factory was where a man with little-to-no education could make a small fortune. The hours were long and grueling, and maybe they'd lose a finger, but in the end they'd bring home enough of that union paper to buy a home in suburbia for their families as well as things for themselves. My father liked to spend his hard-earned dollars on cars, booze, and women.

One day, he brought home a sky blue Thunderbird with matching suede interior and a moon roof. This pissed my mother off. We needed new Buster Browns and clothes for school, and had layaway waiting for us at the K-Mart. My brother and I, however, were thrilled with his purchase. We rode along with him every chance we got, playing tirelessly with the button that made the moon roof open and close until he barked at us to stop. I loved the way my fingertips felt against the blue suede.

Once, my father stopped at a gas station for cigarettes and left the car running while my brother and I waited for him.

"I want to drive." My brother's blue eyes glinted mischievously at me.

"No, Ben," I pleaded with him from the backseat.

"I want to drive," he repeated. Ben was crafty. Just the day before he had built an elaborate climbing structure with toys and chairs that gave him access to the Flintstone's vitamins my mother hid from us in the kitchen.

He eased his way over to the driver's seat, moved the car into neutral and slowly it inched forward. We were driving! Not fast, but driving nonetheless—and headed straight for a wall. There was a crunching thud and my father screamed as we hit the yellow wall of the Bright Horizon's Nursery School next store.

"Don't tell your mother about this," he instructed us. His fear of admitting to her that he'd left her precious babies in a running car outweighed his rage at the scratch on his pride and joy.

It didn't matter much, anyhow. A few months later the car would go missing in the middle of the night. When we asked our father who stole it and if the police would ever bring it back, he would just yell at us to go away.

I didn't realize that my dad was different than anyone else's dad until first grade. June Casey, whose red hair and freckles I was violently jealous of, was my best friend when I started elementary school. She came over for a play date and we spent an afternoon immersed in adventure with our Barbies and Legos. When my dad got home from work, however, June's eyes widened.

"Your dad is black!" she said in disbelief.

I had no idea what she was talking about. I studied him at the dinner table that evening. June was right. How was it that I hadn't noticed before and now it was so obvious? I touched my own hair, course and thick. Not like June's silky hair. She sat next to me and I watched her skinny, freckled arm spoon my mother's Hamburger Helper onto her plate. I hated her. I wanted that milk-like skin. Why couldn't I have that? I was somewhere in between. I was kind of brown. There was no one like me in school. I was a freak. An ugly, frizzy-haired, bucktoothed freak. I pushed my dinner plate away.

Both of my parents were beautiful. My mother, half Italian and half Finnish, never wore a speck of makeup. Her hair, thick and espresso-colored, fell past her waist. My father had a hint of Irish blood that gave him the bluest eyes set against his bronze skin. Two gorgeous people; but I try now to picture them in love with each other and I can't. I try to envision them arm-in-arm and I can't. The idea is completely foreign to me. There are pictures, of course: One of my mother standing next to my father in front of an airplane looking up at him like he's a god. In another, she's two months pregnant with me and beams at the camera from the steps of town hall after their shotgun wedding.

There are pictures of my father and me, too. I am looking at him with the same enchanted look on my face. He holds me in his arms, looking into my eyes that are mirror images of his. There's one at the Detroit Zoo, I'm holding his hand on a vacation in Florida. Yeah. We must have been very happy, all of us, at some point in time. I just wish I could remember it better.

4.

HAD A DAD

I WAS SEVEN OR EIGHT WHEN MY MOTHER moved my brother and I to a two-story house in Detroit. It wasn't our house on Ranch Hill and it certainly didn't have a grapevine or a sandbox, but it did have a laundry chute we could fit in and slide down to the basement and hardwood floors that were slippery under our shoes. We were smitten.

We spent the morning painting the walls of the house with my mother. I chose mauve for my room and my brother chose blue. We didn't ask where my father was or why we were in a strange house in a strange neighborhood. My mother's tired face told us everything we needed to know.

My grandparents came by the new house later that afternoon and we walked from room to room together. My grandpa frowned. Words were spoken in hushed tones between my grandmother and mother in our new kitchen. The next day we took our suitcases and settled into my grandparent's house in Southfield. My mother stayed in the room she grew up in, I was put in my Aunt Katie's room, and my brother settled into my Uncle Cal's room. And that's how it happens.

Divorces are shattering. Your whole life changes overnight. You're carted off to your grandparent's house. Your mother stops smiling and ages 10 years before your eyes. Your father doesn't come around. When he does, it's court ordered and he takes you to miniature golf or loads you up with sweets and toys in attempt to make you forget he's even gone at all. Then he delivers you back to your mother, who is waiting with arms crossed in the front yard and who simply can't compete with a new Herself the Elf play set.

Our father still lived in the house we grew up in. We did not go back to that house for what seemed like a very long time, and then one day we were dropped off for an afternoon with him. We sat in my mother's Escort in the driveway of our old house for a while, pleading with her not to make us go in. It seemed odd to me that the house still existed at all, as if after my brother, mother, and I left it should've crumbled to the ground.

My mother finally shooed us out of the car towards our father who stood waiting in the doorway. Our hellos with him were brief. I eyed the house behind him. There was no laughter echoing through it, no games of Mad Dog to be played, no frogs being pulled apart in the living room. The foyer that had swallowed me whole and broken my ankle now looked timid. The sunshine still made thick, dusty rays through the living room and I took comfort in that as I kneeled in front of the big bay windows that looked out into our backyard. Sandbox. Grapevine. Somehow it was all still there.

"Ice cream?" my father asked. He was always at a loss for what to do with the court-mandated eight hours his two children were left in his care.

I beamed. Food! Food equaled happy feelings. We hopped in my father's van and rode down Telegraph Road to Farrell's, our favorite ice cream joint. Human League played on the stereo as my dad blew smoke rings out the window.

My brother and I sang along in the back of the Ford Astrovan while performing robotic dance moves. Every mile or so, my dad would pull over, hop out, and run behind the van for a crushed can he'd seen in the road.

"Daddy can do!" he'd announce, holding the retrieved can over his head like a trophy after he got back into the van. Michigan's recycling program could make an opportunist a rich man.

We pulled up to Farrell's, pushed our way through the doors, and claimed the big booth. I ordered a butterscotch sundae. I had ice cream. I had my brother. I had my daddy. I was feeling a lot better about things.

Then *she* walked over to us.

She wore a beret, and her big breasts and thighs jiggled under her clothing. My father stood up to greet her.

"This is Angie," he said, putting his arm around

her as she stared at us with glassy eyes. He squeezed her ass and she giggled. I was suddenly very aware of my stomach hanging over my tie-dyed stretch pants, the butterscotch that had coagulated on the corner of my lip, my frizzy hair.

"Hi," Angie squeaked, popping her gum and shifting her weight from hip to hip. She draped herself across my father as her eyes darted back and forth between my brother and me. I looked out Farrell's window at the grey skies and heavy traffic on Telegraph Road. My sundae was no longer appealing.

The ride back home in the Astrovan was quiet and reserved. Back at our old house, I went directly to my bedroom and slammed the door shut. I'd inherited my Aunt Linda's yellow bamboo furniture and my parents had hung matching curtains in my windows. I had previously had intense nightmares sleeping beneath those curtains. My arch nemesis, Big Bird, would come to my window every night in all of his yellow-feathered glory, knock on it with his beak, and ask me if I was asleep yet. The nightmares only ceased when my brother came in before bedtime one evening wielding his He-Man sword at all of my windows.

"LEAVE MY SISTER ALONE!" he had commanded, effectively banishing Big Bird from my tiny kingdom for good. The whole family had slept much better after that.

Most of my favorite things were still in that yellow room. I decided that they needed to come back to my grandparent's house with me immediately. I didn't want this Angie to come by and poke around at my things. I started to pack them up in my back-pack: my dolls, the plush dog I'd named Dodo Bird and had rubbed my vagina on every night to help me fall asleep, my collection of Scandinavian fairy tales. Everything went into the bag. My father walked in and watched silently as I gathered my belongings.

"You don't have to take this stuff now," he whispered. He studied me for a moment more, then yanked the backpack out of my hand and threw it to the floor, scattering Barbie dolls across the carpet. "I said you don't have to take all this shit with you right now," he yelled, his words trailing off into a muffled whimper.

I sat on the edge of the bed and stared at the wall. I wanted him to go away. Where had he been? We'd been waiting weeks for him to see us. Had he been with her? Had my brother, mother, and I been re-placed that easily?

He sat on the bed next to me and his body began to shake. I stiffened. He was crying. I'd never seen my father cry, not even when his father had died. I wanted to reach for him, to curl my tiny body around his. Instead I remained straight-armed and silent. His face fell to his hands in great, heaving sobs, and as he cried, it came to me. The idea happened in an instant, but it was an instant of intense clarity that my young mind was overtaken by. I knew just what to do to fix the situation.

Heart attack, I decided. I had read about this "heart attack" thing in the big blue medical book on my grandmother's shelf. I closed my eyes.

My father was working in the yard, right by our grapevine. I waved to him. He started to wave back at me, then stopped and clutched at his chest. I watched him fall to the ground, the shovel in his hand hitting the earth with a thud. I ran to him, of course... but it was too late. He was gone, just like my grand-daddy. At the funeral, I leaned over his casket and kissed him on the cheek. I put purple flowers on his grave, the kind we used to pick together when I was a kid. I would miss him. But it was better to say goodbye now. Better to end it now.

And just like that, he was dead to me.

5.

BLOOD IS THE BEST LUBRICANT

I WAS 10 YEARS OLD WHEN THE BLOOD came. It stained my underwear and toilet tissue. Sometimes it was brown and sometimes crimson and when it went away it always came back eventually. It was happening. I was dying. I was sure it was cancer. Maybe even leukemia. I'd seen this kid on the news with leukemia. They had wrapped her bald head up with a giant red bow, like she was some sort of rotten Christmas present. I didn't want to go to the hospital and have them shave my head, too. Better not to tell my parents. I didn't want to worry them. They didn't have time to worry about my cancer, anyhow. Instead, when the blood would arrive, I'd wad the toilet paper up into a thick square and put it inside my underwear. I hoped no one else would notice I was dying. It would stay my secret.

"Autumn! Come here!" my mother called to me from the laundry room after I had been dying for about six months. She held a pair of my mauve leggings in her hand, the crotch covered in blood. She had found the cancer.

"You started your period? Why didn't you tell me?" My mother beamed at me. I didn't even know what a "period" was. She took me into her bathroom and thrust a box of pads in my hand. She then unwrapped a voluminous cotton panty liner to demonstrate.

"When you get your period, you put this in your underwear, just like this." She unpeeled double-sided tape from the pad and stuck it on a pair of her underwear. "Want to try?"

I threw the box across the bathroom and marched out of the room. I felt dirty. The fact that I was not dying couldn't and wouldn't console me. This "period" thing was awful, and my mother seemed to be taking extreme pleasure in my pain. My stepfather, Rodney, sat on the couch in the living room in his tighty-whitey underwear, eating his morning bowl of Captain Crunch. Our dog, Snickers, a melancholy Shepherd mix from the pound, sat at his feet with her mouth sealed shut with duct tape—a direct result of her affinity for eating the clay bowls I made in my pottery class. She stared up from her spot on the shag carpet and winced at me. She knew instinctively that I, too, had been silenced.

Rodney nodded at me amidst the deafening mastication of his favorite cereal. I could tell he also knew about the blood. My mother was such a traitor. I kept my head down, Walkman headphones covering my ears, as I made my way to our backyard.

My brother, mother, and I had reclaimed our

original home: 23144 Ranch Hill. Much to my dismay, Rodney had joined us. From the beginning of their relationship, Rodney had been cursed with a series of plagues: He parted his hair down the middle. He wore aviator sunglasses and nylon shorts that hugged his balls. He lived with his mother. He'd killed my grandfather's prized Sharpei, Chang, by leaving the front door open for a fraction too long when picking my mother up on a date. Chang, a fighter by nature, had shoved past him, hot on the trail of a squirrel, and had been immediately hit by a car.

I hated the man. We fought vehemently every day. My mother's hair had begun to fall out in patches, leaving shiny, bald circles on her scalp.

They slept in the same bed that my mother and father had originally used, and then my father and Angie. It made me sick. I couldn't even look at that bed. I preferred to envision it bursting into flames.

I envisioned the whole house bursting into flames as I strolled the perimeter of my sanctuary-no-more, Guns N' Roses blasting in my ears. At least I had Axl Rose! I was sure he'd understand. When had my world become so different? Our precious grapevine had blown down in a storm and our sandbox was overgrown with weeds. My childhood friend, Lee, who had lived to our right and affectionately been called "Flea" by my brother and I, was long gone, as was the old couple that lived to our left, along with their Halloween apples and palm crosses before Easter.

A woman raking the leaves from her adjoining

backyard noticed my stare. She waved at me, pushing thick glasses up her nose, and I took one headphone off my ear as she walked over to me.

"Hi there. You must be my new neighbors." She put one hand on her hip and smiled wide, leaning on her rake. She had no idea I wasn't new. I wasn't new at all.

"Hello." I wrinkled my nose at her.

"Well, I'm glad we've got new folks coming in. The last people that lived here were so loud. They were black... a black guy and his kids." She wiped the sweat from her brow and laughed nervously. "Well, I hope you all won't be so loud. You look like nice folks. Nicer than that black family!"

My cheeks burned. At 10, I was too passive to tell the nosy neighbor to shove her bigotry up her ass. Our city, Southfield, bordered Detroit and there had been an influx of African Americans in the area, causing alarm within the frosty community. Detroit, the good ol' Motor City, was a city not only fueled by gasoline, but by hate. It had been somewhat seg-regated since the race riots of the sixties drew divid-ing lines between the city and suburbia. Old wounds reigned supreme.

In Detroit I was an oddity. When my parents got married, my mother lost friends. When they took my brother and I out in public, we were the subjects of stares and whispers. I didn't understand it until I started school and my brown skin stood out in con-trast next to the lily-white kids from my neighbor-hood and the dark-skinned kids that were bussed in from the city. We didn't fit in.

"Fucking niggers!" some of my white friends would say before remembering I was in the room. "Well, I don't mean you, you're not like *them*," they would add, shrugging.

The black girls in school were relentless in their efforts to break my spirit.

"Do you have lice?" one ringleader would say, pulling my kinky mass of curls. "Honkies have lice, and you're half honky!"

I nodded at the woman, put back on my headphones and turned to look at my house. The pad in my underwear felt bulky and awful. I could see Rodney watching me from the window. I had a wonderful daydream about hacking him to pieces as I walked back towards the house. I giggled at the thought of my mother trying to find a box of sanitary pads big enough to clean up that mess.

A couple nights later my brother and I went to visit my father at his new house. Angie had moved in with him. They had a new green leather couch and plush carpet. My brother, father, and I sat down to watch their TV, a big screen complete with a VCR. Above the TV was a wedding portrait of my father and Angie taken in Las Vegas. Angie, who was now our stepmother, flashed a toothy grin in a frothy white dress. My father hadn't told us he had gotten married. My brother paled next to me. We sat in silence as Angie sashayed in and out of the room in her tight white pants. Hack, Hack, Slash. There was room for her in Rodney's body bag too.

6.

DESTRUCT THE THINGS YOU FUCK

"YOU FEEL SO GOOD," STEVEN SAID. I eased down onto his cock, grabbing his shoulders as I rode him up and down inside his Jeep. The scar on his face was illuminated by the glow of the light behind the First Apostolic Lutheran Church that we were parked next to. I was barely eighteen and Steven was thirty. He played drums while I sang off-key in our local band.

Steven was also married.

He'd explained to me many times that he had married his high school sweetheart and that they'd grown apart. They slept in separate bedrooms. He'd wanted a divorce for quite some time but didn't know how to tell her. I supposed it was a lot easier to just fuck 18-year-old girls in the back of his car.

Steven and I did everything together in spite of the wife that waited at home for him, wanting babies and the whole nine yards. We vacationed together, wore matching Doc Martens, and screwed every chance we got. He even took me to my prom. I wasn't sure whether or not I believed what he told me about his wife, but I wasn't sure that I cared either. I had other men to fill in the gaps.

My mother often accused me of being boy crazy. It started with Danny Hunt, a pock-marked, white trash kid that lived in a dilapidated rental with his mother, brother, and two sisters. He had been held back enough times that his voice had fully changed and hair grew from his chin, but Levey Middle School had let him slide through the cracks and into my sixth grade chemistry class. I sat behind him, admiring how his dirty blonde hair curled around his ears. I wondered how his greasy hair felt.

I loved him desperately. I was eleven. He was fifteen.

Danny smelled different than the other boys, a pungent bouquet of impending manhood. I sat enveloped in his scent throughout fifth period. I wanted to pick the pimples that peeked out of his shirt collar, finger the puka shells that he wore around his neck. I wanted to touch him and smell him up close more than anything. From behind Danny, I was conscious of my breathing. Was I too loud?

One day Danny stopped me in the hallway.

"You wanna go hang out with me?" He looked at me with his yellow eyes and licked his lips. The wolf had smelled the lamb behind him. I was lightheaded under his gaze.

I shrugged my shoulders. We went out to the back of the schoolyard and he pressed me against the wall. I trembled. He put his mouth on mine and slid his tongue in. I wanted to throw up. What was this disgusting sensation? But as he went in for a second time, the upset in my stomach settled. My legs felt wobbly, like they might give.

"Do you want to be my girlfriend?" he asked, hand on my throat. I nodded yes. Danny began to call me on the phone after school every afternoon.

"Are your parents home?"

"No," I'd report, and then he'd pedal his ten-speed over to my house. I'd let him in and he would take me to the bathroom in the additional wing of our house. There was an easy exit to the garage from there in case my parents came home early. He'd turn off the lights, push me into the little shower, and make me lay down on my back while he touched me.

"No one else will ever do this to you," he'd say, and slide his cold tongue between my legs. I squirmed from underneath him. My mother hadn't taught me anything about sex. I didn't know if it was wrong or right. I just knew that I thought about him all the time.

"Now you do it to me," he said, pushing my head down into his lap. "Kiss it. See how far it will go in."

I leaned my head down and opened up wide enough to put his penis in my mouth. His flesh was sticky. I gagged and retracted.

"Good girl," he said. "You can't ever do that to anyone else, and you can't tell you did it to me." He stroked my throat with his hand.

Danny made my mother nervous.

"I never had sex until I was married," she lied after she learned I had a boyfriend. I kept my eyes on the floor. The last thing I wanted to talk to her about was sex. I didn't really want to talk to her at all.

Danny always met me outside the brick entrance to school every morning. One day, he didn't show. I went to my first period class and tried to concentrate but my thoughts centered on him. He still wasn't around after second period. During third period, I was called to the principal's office. As I walked down the hallway my blood ran cold.

I opened the door and my mother and Danny's mother, Cathy, sat in the office chairs. Cathy's face was raw and puffy. My mother looked shell-shocked. They both walked me outside. I felt like I was going to throw up.

We stood in the sun for a moment, and Danny's mother finally spoke.

"Danny was hurt once," she started and paused. "It happened at church. Someone hurt him... so this really isn't his fault. He didn't mean to hurt his sister." My face turned red. I rolled her words around in my brain, trying to make sense of them.

"Danny," my mother interjected, "isn't coming home for a while. He touched his sister and he had to go away." I couldn't breathe. "You are not to talk to him anymore."

I turned away from her stare. "Okay," I said. "I have to go back to class now. I have a test."

"Are you okay?" My mother touched me on the shoulder.

"I'm fine," I said, and pushed her hand away. I

didn't want to be touched.

"Okay, well, we'll talk later about this more?"

"I don't need to." I turned and walked back into school. I went to my locker and took out Danny's notebook. He always left it in my locker when he couldn't open his, which was most of the time. It smelled just like him. I opened it, burying my nose in the pages and breathing him in. I held it in my hands and cried.

The news spread like wildfire through our middle school. By the next afternoon everyone knew that Danny Hunt had been sent away for "diddling" his sister. The kids were unforgiving. Spitballs were launched at my head, laughter thrown in my face. I walked the halls with my head down. I tried to make it through the day without going to the girls' bathroom. When I couldn't hold it in any longer, I found the bathroom furthest away from every class, aware that it would make me late for math class. I snuck behind the sanctuary of the restroom's big red door, locking myself in the last stall.

One time, I was seen. The door slammed open again, letting in two giggling girls.

"He musta had to do that to his sister because you wouldn't fuck him," one said, tapping on my stall door with her nails. I stared at my feet. "You shoulda sucked his dick."

"Nasty bitch," her friend joined in.

I could see their Reeboks under the stall door as they stood and waited for me to come out. I knew the bell would ring any second. I just had to wait for it.

I stopped going to the bathroom altogether after that day. My insides atrophied. My mother took me to the doctor. They poked and prodded me, gave me barium shakes to drink so that they could investigate my intestines on the big screen. I was too ill to go to back to school. I stayed at home, comatose on the couch.

The letters began to arrive. Danny sent me snippets of his hair with letters from prison. Once, he even sent me a piece of his skin. All of his letters smelled like him and I would sleep with them under my pillow. I wanted to be sick forever so I could stay and watch the mailbox.

Danny had an older brother named Todd. Todd was even better looking than Danny and acne free. He also always wore a leather trench coat that I was infatuated with. I decided with Danny long gone, Todd was my next best option. But there were other contenders as well.

From the ninth grade on, I'd had dates booked for breakfast, lunch, and dinner. My mother was beside herself.

"One of these boys is going to kill you," she'd say. "Someone is going to chop you up and put you in a suitcase!"

But how could I choose? I loved them all desperately and for different reasons until they'd do something to annoy me. It could be something as slight as the way they chewed their food, a catch phrase they overused, or a song I loved that they didn't get. Whatever the reason, I would cut them off instantly and brutally, wanting them scarred, all of them. After all, I knew they would do it to me eventually. I had to protect myself. I hated them all.

Even the man underneath me in the parking lot of the First Apostolic Lutheran Church.

Steven sometimes mewed like a cat when he was coming. It had always annoyed me. He closed his eyes, bit the scar on his lip, mewed, and I knew he was finishing. Thank goodness. I climbed off of him, slipped back into my underwear, and laid my head in his lap. Steven clutched my face and smiled.

"Princess, I love you," he said. "We need to talk about something." His mouth pulled to the right when he spoke. "I'm getting a divorce."

I was silent.

"Because I want to be able to marry you." He stroked my hair, eager for my reaction...

I laughed. I laughed until tears rolled down my cheeks.

Steven's eyes glazed over as I laughed and I swore I could see right into his skull. That's how I knew about the aneurism. The artery came loose and I watched it splay all over his brain like a garden hose. It was marvelous, the way that it shot around in the air! He didn't have a chance. I'd go to the funeral. I'd shake his wife's hand, tell her how goddamn sorry I was for her loss. Fuck, I'd even send over a floral arrangement.

I laughed until he dropped me back off at my parent's house.

I hated his fucking guts.

7.

THE NATURAL
Inkster, Michigan

"I'D LIKE TO GET A JOB HERE," I SAID TO the worn, dishwater-blonde woman behind the counter of an entrance booth lined in blinking Christmas lights.

"How old are you?" She raised an eyebrow at me.

"Eighteen!" I smiled and shoved my ID into her hand. A faint smell of mold and bar rot was in the air. My friend Christina, along for moral support, giggled as the woman eyed me.

I was seven years old when I'd first decided I wanted to be a stripper. Pre-separation, my parents had left us with our Aunty Denise for a week while they vacationed in Las Vegas. When they came back, they brought with them a Barbie doll-sized showgirl for me, mounted on a platform. She was dressed in a black sequined unitard with black feathers artfully positioned in her perfectly-coiffed blonde hair. Her lips were pouty, her eyelids painted electric blue. I fell in love with her immediately. Many hours were spent studying the doll; her shiny plastic limbs, lumps of breasts, flawless face stuck in a coquettish expression. She represented everything that I wanted to be and was not: A beauty queen as well as a tiny temptress on a pedestal. I was just a chubby, buck-toothed kid that got in the way of my parents' burgeoning arguments.

In my room, I became my own tiny showgirl with the spotlight on me. I danced just the way I thought she would, thrusting my hips this way and that. I daydreamed that my parents would look in on me, see me dancing, and remember how wonderful I was. They would tell their friends. Maybe they would even take me to Vegas the next time, too, and I'd dance in one of those fancy shows.

They never looked in on me.

Not long after I got my doll, the phenomenon of hair metal was just getting under way. In a few years I'd hear Mötley Crüe's "Girls, Girls, Girls" on the radio, see the video, and be enticed to perform a two-step in the privacy of my yellow pre-teen bedroom. Yes. This is what men wanted. Fast women in heels and lots of makeup. They loved them so much that they stuck them on pedestals and sold them in souvenir shops in Las Vegas.

Finally, I was old enough to become a public object of desire.

"Well, you'll have to audition," the woman said, blowing smoke from the corner of her mouth past my face. "Just because you're cute doesn't mean you don't have to audition like everyone else."

I peered around behind her. It was midday and the bar was almost empty.

"Okay, what do I have to do?" I asked. She pointed a fat, French-manicured nail towards a podium in the corner.

"Go see DJ Mark, pick out a song. Dressing room is in the back. You did bring costumes, right?"

"I... I don't have any yet," I replied, nervously kicking my motorcycle boot against the booth.

"Well, you got a bra and panties on, dontcha?"

I did, and I was grateful that both were fairly clean.

DJ Mark was like a sweatier version of *All in the Family's* Meathead. He looked bored and beaten down by life but when he spoke over the microphone his voice was wet with excitement. "Coming up on stage one we've got BRANDY! And on stage two, SLOOPY!"

I turned to see what the excitement was all about. "Brandy" was a chubby brunette who lacked rhythm and "Sloopy" looked like it was time for a retirement party.

"Dude, she has no tits!" Christina whispered.

I was ecstatic. I didn't have any tits either.

"What are you calling yourself? What's your stage name?" DJ Mark chewed his gum, disinterested in the new girl in front of him. What a concept, to be able to name yourself! To be able to define yourself in one word and escape the mundaneness of the name you were born into. Oh, the possibilities!

And... I couldn't think of a thing.

"Rio," I blurted out. "Like the Duran Duran song." I didn't even like Duran Duran. I also needed to pick a song. Mark had an ample collection of rock 'n roll and I chose Gun N' Roses', "Welcome to the Jungle" as my first strip song.

There I was, 18 years old, in a worn-out bra, panties, and motorcycle boots, making my way to center stage at Henry the Eighth's at two o' clock in the afternoon on a Wednesday. All eyes were on me as I stepped onto the stage. I was fresh meat. They could smell it. The day girls cut their eyes on me as the autoworkers on their lunch breaks whistled. Dishwater's cigarette dangled from her lips as she watched.

I walked up the steps leading to the stage with my hands trembling. My legs felt like they might buckle. There was no pole on the stage... wasn't there supposed to be a pole to hang on to? As the music started, something happened to me. I felt infinite. For the first time, I really didn't care what anybody thought of me. Spinning around in my motorcycle boots, I was finally free. I danced way too fast, more music video than strip club, but I felt fabulous. I got down on my knees and flipped my hair backwards, then crawled across the stage. By the final notes of "Welcome to the Jungle" at least twelve crumpled dollars lined my stage. Gas money! I hopped off stage and went back to the DJ booth where Mark and Dishwater were conspiring.

"So, you haven't ever danced before?" he asked.

"No." I shrugged my shoulders. Had I been awful?

"Well, I guess that makes you a natural born

stripper." He winked at me.

That was the best thing that I had ever heard.

"If you want to work tonight be back at eight," Dishwater said.

"Yes, ma'am!"

"And don't call me ma'am. I work for a living!"

It seemed like eight o'clock would never come. I felt my life was about to begin in that bar and every second I sat on my parents' couch was a second that I could be making money. As I stepped through the doors to Henry's at 7:55, Dishwater was still on her stool chain smoking, but this time she smiled at me as I handed her my twenty-dollar shift fee.

The night girls weren't as easy to get along with as the day girls who stared but were too weary to lament much over my presence. As I made my way to the closet-sized changing room, strippers in various shades of undress flashed me looks of death.

"You have to fucking wait, there's no goddamn room in here!"

"Change in the bathroom, you idiot!"

"Close the door, my fucking pussy is hanging out!"

Feeling traumatized within the first five minutes of my shift, I retreated to the bathroom, a two-stall (one with no door) filth garden with a cracked mirror. Two older women, Kat and Shawnee, were in there getting ready as well. Kat was the first person I'd ever seen with fake breasts—after all, it was Detroit. They were lopsided and the left one had a strange indent. Deep red horizontal scars marked the folds of each breast. Nevertheless, being about as flat-chested as one could possibly be, I was quite taken by them.

I quickly changed into my outfit for the evening—a green day-glow bikini and my trusty black motorcycle boots. The other girls looked like pros in their sparkly costumes, heels, makeup, and wigs, but I had naïveté and youth on my side.

I wandered around on the floor of the club, not quite sure what to do with myself. Dancing on stage and flashing my tits at an eager crowd of factory workers was the easy part. Chatting them up and getting them to commit to a lap dance or two was the challenge. All around me, the other girls threw themselves on customers' laps, feigning interest in the most hideous of men. They talked loudly, threw back their heads and laughed at the jokes the men told, stroked their faces and egos, and if they got further, their cocks in the lap dance room. I was shy. I rarely talked to anyone face-to-face. *How was I going to do this?*

"You going to just stand there all night?" An Indian man remarked, noting my look of terror.

"It's my first night, I really don't know what to do," I replied.

It turned out that telling an avid strip-club-goer that it's your first night as a peeler is like telling a frat boy you're a virgin. The man's eyes popped at the prospect of being the recipient of my first professional lap dance ever.

"I'm Basil."

He grabbed my hand and led me to a private room off the DJ booth that housed ten chairs—five on one side of the wall, five on the other. I looked around me to see what the other girls were doing. They mounted their customers, frontwards and backwards, rubbing their crotches and ass cheeks on the men's laps in simulated lovemaking motions. One girl was on her knees, breasts sandwiched between her customer's thighs, as the man's eyes rolled back in ecstasy. I noticed that every girl had her own pace. Some were like jack rabbits, and their customers gripped their chairs for dear life as the girls bounced up and down on top of them. Others were slow and sensual.

"What are you looking at, bitch?" a hard-looking brunette in black vinyl snapped at me.

I averted my eyes and turned to face my customer, deciding to go the slow, sensual route. I peeled off my bikini top and grazed his cheeks with my breasts, then mounted him front ways and began to grind my crotch against his jeans. His cock stiffened and a wave of repulsion surged through me. I tried to stand, but he grabbed my hips and held me down against his cock. *Twenty dollars a song,* I repeated in my head, *twenty dollars a song...*

I got five dances from Basil, which warmed me up for the rest of the crowd. Over the course of the evening I grew accustomed to the feeling of grinding against a stranger's erect, clothed penis. It was easier if I mounted them backwards so that I didn't have to look at their faces. I convinced myself it was just like junior high dry-humping.

After work I was sweaty and tired but exuberant. I drove over to the gas station where Christina worked the midnight shift.

"How was it?" she screeched. "Tell me everything!"

I walked over to her nonchalantly and threw my sweaty wads of cash from the evening into the air. We giggled and scrambled for it on the floor, unraveling the crumpled bills and counting them out.

"One hundred and eighty dollars!" I said triumphantly. It might not have been much by stripper standards, but it was more than either of us could make in a whole week at the gas station back then.

"When are you going back?" Christina asked. We both knew I was hooked.

8.

THE VETERAN

WITHIN A COUPLE OF WEEKS, I WAS A full-fledged Stripperella. Glossy six-inch platform acrylics replaced my Wild Pair motorcycle boots after Dishwater complained that I was leaving scuffmarks all over the main stage. It was a change for the better. My five-foot-two frame was instantly elongated and my butt stuck out like I was a Nigerian track star. I bought new costumes in bright, man-eating colors and changed my name to "Ty." I even bought a long, curly fall—an ingenious half-wig that leaves part of your own hair free—so my hair grazed my ass cheeks.

For the first time in my life I felt like I was a natural part of something. When I walked into the dressing room each night and put on a velvet bikini, I became an elite member of a rag-tag crew of women that had a code and a mission. The girls that worked at Henry's fascinated me. Justice was a freakishly-tall farm girl that could've been a runaway model if she'd been born in New York City instead of Milford,

Michigan. She only danced to Metallica and could do a sideways split with one leg on the stage and another on the ceiling. One night, a customer gave Justice a baggie of drugs. She sniffed it all down and began to foam at the mouth. Her long legs flopped around the room. The paramedics came and took her away, but she was back doing her sideways splits the very next evening.

Summer was a mini version of Tina Turner. She had tight little thighs that she always strapped her cash to with a dirty white garter. The only sign of her having four kids at home was revealed when she took off her top and let loose two shriveled, brown, tube sock breasts. Summer also had raging hemorrhoids. She bent over in front of me one day and noted my interest.

"What, you've never had anal sex?" she snapped.

I hadn't.

Wendy was a ditzy drunk that the waitresses claimed used to be gorgeous. She couldn't have been more than twenty-five, but drinking herself into oblivion every night had taken a toll on her face. Wendy turned tricks after work for one customer, an old businessman who always came to Henry's dressed in a three-piece suit. Sometimes she would leave with him in the middle of her shift and come back to finish the night. One night we were crowded in the dressing room. Wendy was her usual annihilated self and pulled her panties aside.

"That guy gave me warts... Look, it's like a little pink raisin!"

We didn't see Wendy too much after that.

One thing that could break our posse was a regular customer. In the beginning, I wasn't privy to all the unwritten strip club rules. I was schooled by a veteran in a Venus swimwear bikini. When I started working at Henry's, I thought Brooke was the prettiest girl there. She had French tipped nails and long, scrunched hair, reminiscent of Candice Cameron's during the early days of *Full House.* She had breast implants that she had to fly to Utah for, a taut little butt, and was always tan. When she tanned, she left a little foil Playboy Bunny sticker on her hip, so that everyone could see just how far along she had come.

Brooke wouldn't talk to me at first. She was solely a weekend girl and made her grand entrance around seven p.m. on Friday nights. She always wore her catalogue-ordered Brazilian bikini bottoms in fluorescent orange, pink, or yellow, and topped them off with a tiny white tank top sliced to showcase her fabulous under-boob cleavage. She wore an occasional flower in her overwhelming mass of curls. Brooke had regulars that came to see just her. Her dance card was almost always full.

One Friday evening, after Brooke had meandered away from one of her regulars with her customary glass of champagne, he waved me over.

"Are you new here?" he asked, giving me a curious once-over. "I haven't seen you before. Sit with me."

"I've been here a few weeks," I replied as I sat on the bar stool next to his.

"Well, you're beautiful and I think you should

dance for me." He escorted me back to the private lap dance area, where we stayed for fifteen songs in a row. That meant an easy three hundred bucks for me without having to hustle it from multiple customers. I emerged from the lap dance area ecstatic and bumped right into Brooke. Her face twisted when she saw who I had just been dancing with.

Later that evening, she followed me to the payphone in a tiny private area at the back of the club, locking the door behind us.

"Who the fuck do you think you are?" she asked, acrylic nails tapping on the wall, face reddening. "You stole my customer. You saw me sitting with him and you purposely went over to him and stole him."

"He called me over," I said, leveling myself for a fight.

"Bullshit! You're a liar!" Brooke looked like a crazy woman, eyes bulging as she grabbed the payphone off its cradle and aimed it at me. "I want half that money or I'm going to beat the shit of you!"

"Fuck you!" I said. Brooke lunged at me just as Dishwater appeared in the little oval window of the door to the phone booth. She pounded on the door and Brooke reluctantly unlocked it after flashing me a look that seethed, *you lucked out this time, bitch.*

"Brooke, you're suspended for a month. Put your clothes on and get the fuck out of here!" Dishwater bellowed. She didn't get up off of her stool often, but when she did, she meant business.

Brooke let out a tiny cry of discontent before shoving past me.

"She's just mad because she's not the queen bee around here anymore." Dishwater said, winking at me.

9.

CHESTER, CHESTER CHILD MOLESTER

MY FIRST REGULAR WAS A BEATEN-DOWN old man with papery skin the color of a well-used ashtray. I'd noticed him at Henry the Eighth's a few times. He'd come in, order a beer, and keep his head low as he made his way to his favorite seat near the back of the bar. He'd sit for hours, cupping his beer with his papier-mâché hands, face shielded by the shadow of a Detroit Tigers baseball cap. The strippers ignored him. He looked and smelled broke. Late shifters from the steel plants were a better option than the wallflower melting into the scenery.

On a particularly slow night when I had nothing to lose, I approached him for the first time. His eyes perked up as I sat down next to him. They were cornflower blue and shined brightly against his sallow complexion.

"I see you here a lot," I said. "You never talk to anyone."

"Oh, I don't think anyone would really care about anything I have to say," he said.

"Don't sell yourself short."

"Well... I'm Chester," he said.

"I'm Ty, nice to officially meet you." Maybe the other girls had been right. This guy was too meek for a ride in the back and I didn't have time to waste on a chump. I hadn't even made my house fee yet.

"So, how about a dance?" I batted my eyes at him. Chester eyed me up and down.

"You're so pretty... how can I say no?"

I was almost shocked at his agreement to my proposition. I grabbed him by the hand and led him to the VIP area.

I gave Chester 10 dances that night... a good score for a first run with a customer. I made sure to exchange phone numbers with him so that I could tell him when I was working. From that day on, Chester came in to Henry's every time I worked. We would always do at least ten dances, sometimes twenty. When I wasn't dancing for him, he watched me as I walked around the room, propositioning other clients.

"What's your deal?" I asked him one day.

"What do you mean?"

"I mean, do you have a family? Kids?"

Chester looked down at his beer. I felt like an asshole as soon as the words left my mouth. It wasn't my business.

"My wife left me. I haven't seen my kid in years."

"I'm sorry. I shouldn't have asked."

"It's okay." He hesitated and then looked into my eyes. "I was in trouble."

"What kind of trouble?" My curiosity was piqued. Chester just didn't reek of trouble. Was he a bank robber? Grand theft auto?

"I was accused of touching a girl that lived next to us. But I didn't do it. I swear." He twisted on his stool. "Do you believe me?"

It was the last thing I expected out of his mouth. I tried to picture Chester putting the moves on a neighbor kid.

"I don't know," I looked away from him. Chester barely touched *me*, even when he paid for it. But that wasn't something that people usually lied about.

"You're actually nicer to me than my own daughter ever was," Chester said softly.

"Well, I see you more than I ever saw my own father, so we're kind of even." I giggled and grabbed his hand, holding it in mine.

"Would you do something for me?" he asked, squeezing my hand. "Would you have dinner with me one night? I haven't had dinner with anyone in so long."

Ugh, I thought to myself. This was the moment all the girls complained about. The customer asks you out and it's a double-edged sword... If you say no, they think you're a stuck up cunt that they've been blowing their money on, at which point, they stop giving you any business. But if you say yes, you run the same risk. The customer gets attached on your "dates" and all of a sudden you're a faux girlfriend. And we all knew that girlfriends went home full of steak dinner, but *not* with a roll of twenties in their pocket. That's when the idea popped into my head.

"Well... if we have dinner I'd miss part of work and I can't afford that so..."

"I'll pay you," he said in matter-of-fact tone. I was stunned. It was that easy.

The next day before work I met Chester at a roasted chicken joint. He waved to me from across the diner. I smiled and waved back, immediately conscious of what the other patrons would think of this harlot dining with a man three times her age. I changed my gait by pretending the gray-haired man I was making a beeline for was my sweet ol' granddad.

"You're even prettier in the real world," he said, staring at me as I slid into the booth next to him.

"What do you mean *real world*? The club is the real world, too. It's not, like, a parallel universe!"

"No, no, it's different. A girl like you would never talk to me in the real world."

At the end of dinner, he shoved a wrinkled hundred-dollar bill in my hand. I had made lots of hundred dollar bills in the short time I'd been a stripper, but this one was special. It was intoxicating to know that someone had paid me to sit and have a conversation with them.

I started spending more time outside of the club with Chester. We had dinner dates, met up for ice cream, and when I needed groceries, he met me and bought them for me. Our meetings always ended with a hundred in the palm of my hand.

"Oh, Chester, you shouldn't! But I do have that electric bill due..."

10.

PINK FLAMINGOS

JUST OUTSIDE THE GATES TO THE FLAMIN-
go Mobile Home Park on Middlebelt Road, two
stoic pink birds held watch, promising that summer would eventually come despite the most frigid
of winters. Chester called the Flamingo home. Every
spring, tornadoes would rip through the joint and
crater-skinned families would lament over their loss-
es on the five o'clock news. I'd passed by its campy
front entrance many times in my youth without a
reason to venture in. But on that particular day, I was
armed with a box of chocolate-brown hair dye and a
mission.

Chester had been complaining that he looked
like an old man. His ex-wife had dyed his hair in the
past, but since the accusation of diddling, he hadn't
had anyone do it for him. Ever the stripper-with-the-
heart-of-gold, I volunteered to do it for him at his
house, bringing along Christina for safety.

Chester greeted Christina and I at the door.
Besides the fact that it had a 50:50 chance of being
blown away in a storm, the mobile home wasn't so

bad. He had a front porch, two wood paneled bed-rooms, a living room with a tiny TV and a full kitch-en—all swimming in a deep blue carpet.

"You can live here with me," he said as he gave us the grand tour. "I mean if you ever needed to."

"Thank you, Chester. I'll remember that." I looked down at the floor, almost able to picture us taking care of each other.

I colored his hair in his kitchen sink and trimmed it where it looked shaggy around his ears while Christina laughed at *Sanford and Son* on the mini TV. After I dried his hair, I put a drop of pomade in it and led him to the bathroom mirror.

"Close your eyes till we get there," I instructed. "Now open!"

Chester looked into the mirror and welled up with tears. He looked like a completely different per-son. His blue eyes sparkled.

"Thank you," he said, putting his arms around me. He held on for a long time, his body shaking against mine. When he let go, he peeled two hundred-dollar bills out of his pocket and placed them in the palm of my hand.

"I can't believe he gave you two hundred bucks for nothing," Christina laughed on the way home. "He could've gone to the best salon in town for half that. What a chump!!"

"Yeah, what a chump," I echoed, staring out at the falling snow. But I couldn't help but think of how happy he looked when he saw his new reflection. I hoped he was going to get a good night's sleep.

What a chump...

11.

NUMB AND DUMB

SECRET WAS THE KIND OF GIRL WHO spoke with a Southern drawl though she probably hadn't ever been anywhere near the south. Her blonde hair was cropped close to her head. Night after night, her uniform of choice was a yellowed wife beater tank top cut into two jagged pieces—a top for her small, sagging breasts and a matching skirt. Everyone was afraid of Secret, including me.

One day, she cornered me in the dressing room at Henry's.

"You know that Pete and I have us a little family, right?" Her hands were planted firmly on her waist. Pete was the night security at Henry's. He dated Secret but fooled around with a number of the girls. I had absolutely no interest in the menacing-looking brother that loved to slap me on the ass when his lady friend wasn't watching. "I'm just letting you know because I've seen the way that you look at him."

I let out a guffaw. She obviously didn't know my taste in men; long-haired and starch white was my flavor. Her hands remained on her hips but her voice had quivered when I'd made eye contact with her. She knew the truth. She knew she could kick my ass up and down the street but it wouldn't make any difference in the world if her man wanted *me*. Him wanting me would fucking kill her.

"I know that, and I would never take that away from you. He obviously loves you." I enjoyed watching the club bully sweat in front of me and realized I was quickly climbing the power ranks at Henry the Eighth's.

Secret masked the look of relief in her eyes. "Well, I just wanted to tell you in case you didn't know." Her blue eyes softened. "You wanna do a line with me?" She divvied up two lines of coke on the ledge in front of the dressing room mirror. I'd never done coke. I didn't even drink.

"Like this," she said, then snorted a line through a rolled up twenty dollar bill, and handed it over to me. I sniffed up a line and waited for the miracle to come.

"I don't feel anything," I said.

She laid out two more lines. I snorted another back.

"Oh!" My nose burned. Secret laughed.

"Wait till you taste the drip, girl," she said. "That's my favorite part."

My heart raced. I was onstage next. I felt everyone's eyes burning through my skin as I approached the stage. *Did I look different? Could they tell I was high?* I was hyper-aware of my surroundings. Secret smiled at me from across the room. A waitress shot daggers at me. The drip rolled down my throat as I climbed the stairs to stage one. *One foot in front of the other*, I mouthed to myself.

As I danced, the questions went away and I felt electric. Was it just me or was I extra *on* tonight? The crowd hooted and hollered as I spun in my heels. I got a glimpse of myself in the long mirror that was grubby with ass prints across the room from the main stage. I was young and beautiful and people wanted me. They wanted me so much that they gave me twenty-dollar bills to ride their jeaned cocks for two minutes of a RATT song. It was glorious. I would need more of this magic powder.

Secret introduced me to a drug dealer named Waldo who would set up shop at Henry the Eighth's every Friday and Saturday night. Us girls spent our weekends playing a game of "Where's Waldo?" and taking turns saddling up to him, pretending to give him a table dance while he exchanged our ragged twenty dollar bills for baggies of cocaine.

My love affair with cocaine was in full swing. I adored the burn in my nostrils and the following euphoria that coursed through my veins. As long as I was high, I didn't feel anxious or depressed. It felt so good that I didn't want to work without getting lit anymore, and since I worked 6 days a week, doing blow was a daily habit. My new best friend and confidant.

The bully had gotten one over on me after all.

12.

LET'S TAKE THIS SHOW ON THE ROAD

"THIS PLACE IS LIKE A GIANT GREY SLUSHY that no one wants to drink," I said to my brother, staring out the window of his pickup truck. It was wintertime and the snow made silver shadows over a soot-covered Detroit as we drove down Telegraph Road. "I'm going to move to Los Angeles."

My words were matter-of-fact and I believed them as soon as they came out of my mouth. I watched the old Fords that putted by us, unaware that there were places that wouldn't rust their underbellies. I was smitten with my own idea. "I'm going to move to Los Angeles and get the biggest breast implants I can find, call up *Playboy* magazine, and pose naked."

Ben's blue eyes filled with tears.

"Don't talk like that," he said. "What's wrong with you?"

Ben didn't know I was a dancer. None of my family or friends, save my confidant, Christina, knew. I'd been keeping it my little secret. There were two of me now: The Autumn that went to art school and played in a local rock band, and the girl who put on her fake hair and stilettos at night and called herself Ty. It was getting hard to keep my alter ego pinned down to the late night shift.

Ty and I decided that Detroit was too small for us at age 20. A local paper had done a write-up on my band and called me a genuine talent. I was going to move to California. Find a rock 'n' roll band. Maybe even Axl Rose. Christina was beside herself. We had been living in an apartment in Redford for the last few years and my departure meant a move back to her parent's house for her. The night before I left, I had one last chicken dinner with Chester and bought an eight ball from Secret's new boyfriend, a shifty-eyed dealer named Ray. The next morning I packed up my Ford Probe, had breakfast with my mother, and started my drive across the country to Los Angeles to see what I could make of myself and my "genuine talent."

I took the southern route to California. It was four days of driving fueled by Subway sandwiches and hits of cocaine off of my bullet. I dodged herds of buffalo, navigated hailstorms in New Mexico, and pulled into the city in the middle of the night. As I exited the 101 freeway and stepped out of my car onto Sunset Boulevard, my skin tingled with excitement underneath the street lamps. Los Angeleez! I'd made it to the City of Fallen Angels. I had no idea where I was going to live or what I was going to do and I didn't care. My mother, who I'd left waving behind me in a Coney Island parking lot, thought I'd turn around and come right home. I knew I wouldn't.

The first thing I noticed about Los Angeles was that no one noticed me. I mean, they looked, but not with the concrete stares I was used to getting from people in Detroit. In Los Angeles, there were so many different kinds of people doing so many different things that it wouldn't have mattered if I were purple, spoke Swahili, and looking for a career bending spoons. There in the smog, with all the misfits and oddballs, I could finally breathe!

I spent all the money I had saved on a deposit and first month's rent for a North Hollywood apartment. With only enough gas and food money left for a day or so, I needed to find a job immediately.

Stripping in LA was going to be different. They had nude bars. Bars where men drank eight-dollar orange juices and watched gyrating vaginas.

Early on a Wednesday afternoon, I pulled up to the Body Shop on Sunset Boulevard. I sat curbside in my Probe, staring at the bubble-gum breasts advertised on the club's marquee, mustering up the strength to go in. I took a sniff off of my bullet and gathered my dance bag. Music boomed inside the near-empty club. A couple of old strippers hunched around the bar while two or three customers in rumpled business suits looked sullenly at their exorbitant glasses of juice. The manager showed me the dressing room, lingering as I procured a lacy white outfit from my stripper bag.

"How old you?" he asked in a thick Persian accent, leaning against the door.

"Old enough," I said, closing the door in his face.

I slipped on my white outfit and looked at myself in the mirror. My legs were bruised from the cocaine as well as the poor diet and my skin was bad from traveling. But I was in Hollywood on the Sunset Strip! I painted on my favorite red lipstick and posed for myself.

The Persian rapped on the dressing room door.

"You up now!" he said, leading me to the DJ booth at the front of the runway-style stage.

"Can you play 'Girls, Girls, Girls' for me by Mötley Crüe?" I asked the DJ. He gave me the once-over and rolled his eyes at my choice, but the motorcycle intro burst into the room regardless of his distaste for it.

The stage was smooth and glassy, a far cry from the scuffed dance floors at Henry the Eighth's back home. I grasped the pole for support, knees shaking as I repeated a lame semi-circle around it. *Fuck this*, I thought to myself. The last thing I needed was a broken leg. I got down on all fours and crawled across the stage in the direction of the rumpled suits. A young thing in their presence had awakened their libidos. They limped over in a pack, practically salivating at my little mosquito bites peeking out from behind pristine lace. I'd forgotten that I had to drop trough as well. The suits held back their dollars in anticipation of the big payoff. I laid on my back, lifted my legs, and shimmied the fabric off, struggling as my g-string got caught on my heel, However, an exposed vagina apparently excused all failed attempts at gracefulness. Dollar bills fluttered around me.

That wasn't so bad, I thought to myself, mentally calculating my lunch and gas money as I gathered my clothes back up. I waved goodbye to the tiny, whistling crowd, and made my way back to the dressing room. I was stepping into my jean shorts when a seasoned brunette threw the door open.

"I had a hundred dollar bill in here that you stole from me!" she bellowed at me, her words soaked in vodka.

"What are you talking about? I was only in here for five minutes and I didn't see any money."

"Fucking liar!" she screeched, lunging at my purse. I swung backwards and she fell flat on her face, adding to her infuriation. "I'll fucking kill you, bitch, I fuck with rappers that will kill you!" She crawled her way up and lunged again when the Persian ran in.

"Jasmine, get the fuck out of here or I fire you now!" he roared at her. Jasmine winced at his words, retreating like a broken old horse to the club floor. I caught my breath while he apologized.

"These girls, you know... they crazy when they drink." It was noon. The Persian knew I wouldn't be back. "Try my cousin's club, you like it there," he said, handing me a business card. "I tell him you coming!"

The card directed me to a club on Hollywood Boulevard called Cheetahs. When my eyes adjusted from the blaring California sun to the din of the strip bar, I saw a petite redhead hanging upside down from a center-stage pole like gorgeous, suspended art. The Persian's cousin had been expecting me. I was hired and put on the schedule for that very night.

My shift started at 8 p.m. The girls were genuine performers at Cheetahs. A tall, skinny black girl with violet contact lenses was on stage. I watched in awe as she climbed to the top of the pole, spread her legs on it lengthwise and spun all the way down spread eagle. I couldn't do pole tricks like that! I was certain I'd be laughed off of the stage.

I ducked into the bathroom to put on my favorite velvet bikini and took a courage hit off my bullet. My hands trembled and it tumbled to the ground, shattering on the tile floor, a hot mess of glass and cocaine. The girl in the stall next to me poked her head under.

"You drop, you share," she said. She got on all fours and craned her head under the stall, forming a line with her fingers. I stared forlornly at the last of my Detroit cocaine disappearing up the crouching stripper's nose. With no idea where I'd get more, I briefly considered scooping some of the remnants up. *How bad could a little glass and grime be?*

"All yours," I said, and stepped out.

Stripped of my powdered courage, I had to drum up some tenacity to get through my first set of the night. *So what if I was pole deficient?* The dancers at Cheetahs were full of tricks but scowled as they performed. I had a 50,000-watt smile to draw the dollars in. I'd use that.

I had the DJ play the first song I had ever stripped to, "Welcome to the Jungle," and I danced across the stage, shaking my hair around like a rock star. Dollar bills hit me from all angles, and when I got off-stage I had offers for lap dances waiting. At the end of the night I'd banked one hundred and thirty dollars, which was a far cry from my Henry the Eighth's six-hundred-dollar nights. But it was something. And me? I was going to be okay.

13.

THAT NEW HAIR FEELING

A ROACH CRAWLED ACROSS THE CEILING directly over my head. I opened my eyes just in time to see him scurry and linger over my makeshift bed. I grabbed a sneaker and threw it up towards the insect as hard as I could. The roach fell to the ground beside me and I flicked it across the room, making a mental note to put bug spray on my shopping list. What did a roach want with my new apartment anyway? There was no food there.

I sat up in my sheets and stretched out. I had no furniture, but I was in Hollywood! Well, North Hollywood, and the California sun warmed my body through my open blinds. It was Wednesday. Wednesdays meant 39-cent cheeseburgers at McDonald's, and if I was really lucky, I would peel the mystery prize sticker off of my soft drink and have a shot at 11-cent French fries. I would eat like a queen.

I curled back up in the nest of old blankets I'd made on my floor, thinking about the salty goodness that would be mine, when a wave of thick nausea rolled over me. I stood up to run to the bathroom and found my legs wobbling beneath me. A foot from the bathroom my body gave out. Green projectile vomit sprayed the hallway. I slumped against the wall, sweating. *Fuck.* I was going to have to clean that up.

I inspected my vomit from a safe distance. Thai food. I'd splurged on sweet-and-sour chicken the day before because it had reminded me of a place I used to eat in Detroit with Ben. Goddamn Thai chicken. I crawled back to my nest, carpet scratching my bruised stripper knees. The vomit clean-up could wait. It would crust over and be easier to clean up. As soon as I made it back to my blankets, the sickness rose up again. I made a second pilgrimage to the bathroom and decided it best to stay there with my face pressed against the cool linoleum.

When I was a little girl I caught things that no one else did, like whooping cough, scarlet fever, and mono. My mother would sing to me and have me suck on a wet rag so I wouldn't get too dehydrated. I wished she was there to take care of me. I wanted to tell her to come, to get on a plane and take care of me. I wanted to tell her that I was sorry about everything I'd turned out to be and that I'd be different. But I knew I couldn't call her. I couldn't let her know I needed her, that I was weak. No one should ever know that. I'd made it this far alone. I lurched up and grabbed the edge of the toilet bowl, puked up some more clear bile, and fell asleep on the dirty bathroom floor.

I woke up stiff, birds singing through the night

sky to me through my window. The birds sang at night in California! I'd never heard them sing at night at home. I lifted myself up on my elbows, sore from the bathroom floor. My mouth tasted like a tin cup. I limped out into the living room where my clock radio flashed neon green: 11:14 p.m. I'd been asleep nearly 15 hours and I was two hours late for my shift at Cheetahs.

"FUCK!" I grabbed my crumpled jeans from the floor, fished through the pockets for the business card they'd given me, and dialed the number. "Can I speak to Raffi?"

"This him."

"This is Ty; I just started yesterday?"

"Where are you, babe? You're late."

"I'm so sorry I didn't come in, but I have food poisoning and I..."

"Listen, honey, lots of girls want to work here. You can't call in two hours late. Why don't you come back in two weeks? Maybe we rehire you then." Click.

Two weeks? I couldn't survive two weeks on the money I had left. Tears welled in my eyes. I'd have to find another place to work, and fast.

I opened my purse, looking for my bullet of cocaine before remembering the previous night's misadventure in the bathroom. Jobless, furniture-less, and even drug-less. I wasn't sure what hurt the most. At least the food poisoning had subsided. I was hungry. I got into my Ford Probe and headed for the nearest McDonald's.

"Two cheeseburgers, please," I said to the pregnant Mexican girl behind the counter. I took them to go and parked next to the 101 freeway under the big white cross that overlooks Hollywood and the San Fernando Valley. I closed my eyes as I chewed and pretended that the sound of the traffic was really waves crashing on the beach.

I woke up the next morning thoroughly dejected by my situation and decided that the only cure was new hair. New hair is a magical thing for a stripper. 24 inches of synthetic fibers fashioned into luxurious locks could transform a listless attitude into a sex bomb tornado. With fresh hair I'd be a relentless money-making machine that would make the women at the next club cower in fear and cling to their regulars. I envisioned myself in a honey-blonde wig.

Yes, I would become a California blonde!

I counted out the remainder of my money. I had exactly $126.53. A wig would cost me roughly $80.00, leaving me with $46.53 until I could get another job. Minus $20.00 for a baggie of coke... *if* I could find a new dealer. I'd then be down to $26.53. I could make that work. With my budget figured out, I headed to the new hair store.

The wig store was a candyland of fantasy. Elegant foam heads with perfect noses and lips boasted the latest hairstyles in rich reds, ash blondes and chocolate browns. The synthetic wigs were the cheapest, but you couldn't put any heat on them. High on the shelves were the real deal—wigs made of human hair harvested from China, Russia, and even Italy. The thought of wearing some exotic Italian bird's hair made me smile. I pictured myself sipping espresso on a European street with raven ropes of hair cascading down my shoulders. When I opened my eyes, there was a man across the store staring at me intently. I put my head down and fingered the silky blonde strands of the wig in front of me. The man waddled over. He was portly and his pants were too tight. His belly filled the front of them, the zipper begging for mercy.

"Are you an actress?" he asked, pushing his thick glasses up a greasy nose. "You look like an actress."

"Yes," I stammered. "I mean, I haven't done anything yet, but I'm going to get an agent and start getting work."

"Well, I'm a director... would you be interested in doing a video for me?"

I couldn't believe my luck. "Sure... what kind?"

"Have you done fetish?" His smile revealed yellow teeth, tartar building up in the crevices.

My face flushed hot red. "I don't do porn," I said, pushing past him.

"It's not porn, it's fetish. Food fetish. It's easy. Look, I'll pay you five hundred dollars and I'll buy you this wig you seem to like."

I turned around to find him holding the foam head with the silky blonde wig. I thought about the $26.53 I had calculated.

"Okay. But you pay me first," I said, pulling my shoulders back. "As soon as I get there."

"Fine, and you don't get your wig till you get

there," he said.

"Deal."

"I'm Joel." He shook my hand, flashing me his tartar teeth again.

Two days later, I parked in front of the Madilyn Clark rehearsal studios on Burbank Boulevard, with stripper shoes and a bikini in a bag next to me. I headed into Studio C as I'd been instructed. The door was open and a cheap-looking video camera was set up on a tripod. Plastic wrap was stretched across the floor and a fold-up table was set up like a lunch buffet catered by Costco. I wanted to turn around but Joel had already seen me. He shuffled over and handed me five crisp hundred-dollar bills and my blonde wig. Both felt too good in my hands to turn around and walk away, though I was half afraid that I'd end up suffocated and wrapped in the plastic wrap by the end of the shoot. I mentally planned a quick escape route and left my car keys and purse within quick reach before fastening on my new hair.

Once in my bikini, Joel directed me to stand on the plastic tarp. I stepped onto it gingerly.

"Rub yourself, look sexy," he said from behind his camcorder.

I ran my hands up and down my body and pouted my lips. *This isn't so bad,* I thought to myself. I didn't have to show my tits, and I was almost unrecognizable with the platinum wig covering my brown hair. I turned around and swayed side to side. Joel walked to the table, picked out a lemon meringue pie, and brought it to me.

"Now slowly rub this all over."

I took the pie and smashed it against my breasts coquettishly, then spread it all over my body. Joel looked pleased and brought me over another pie, Boston cream. This was going to be the easiest five hundred dollars I had ever made. I slithered around on the plastic wrap, covered in dessert. Next, Joel brought over a carton of eggs. I cracked them in my hands and rubbed them on my tits and ass.

"On your face," Joel commanded from behind the camera. I frowned, sure that I'd be leaving with salmonella poisoning. I rubbed the raw egg on my face and slid it down my arms. Joel was ecstatic.

"Two-minute break!" he said giddily.

I sat cross-legged on the plastic tarp as he went to work with a can opener on an industrial-sized container. He carried the container over to me, belly bulging in high water khakis.

"I'm going to have to pour this over you," he said, huffing from the weight of the container. He tilted it and a healthy stream of shit-brown baked beans hit my chest and belly.

I wanted to retch as the smell of molasses, ketchup, and onions coagulated in my noise. The beans cemented on my now-tarnished blonde wig and my neck, barbecue juices pooled in the crotch of my bikini.

I was going to be sick.

"Smile and pose!" Joel waved his hand around like he was directing a summer blockbuster.

I feigned a weak smile and did a 360, slipping in

the beans. They squished between my toes, and Joel, delighted, got a close-up for the foot and foodie aficionados.

"I'm going to go take a leak and then we have another pie! Chocolate! You're doing great!" Joel hummed as he headed to the bathroom, pants crawling up his rear.

The thought of adding the smell of chocolate to the baked beans was more than I could bear. My stomach gurgled. I hadn't heard a toilet flush yet, so I guessed that I had about two minutes to put my exit plan into action. I threw my jean shorts and tank top on, grabbed my shoes, purse and keys, and ran barefoot, covered in pie, raw eggs and baked beans, to my car. My hands slipped on the steering wheel as I started her up, made an illegal U-turn on Burbank, and sped home.

14.

STUPID KID

I HAD A FRESH WAD OF CASH IN MY POCKET. Sure, there was a chance that my baked-bean extravaganza would end up in adult video stores somewhere, but the cash in my pocket felt thick and nice against my leg. The other nauseating details could soon be forgotten. I bought toiletries, groceries, and a *Music Connection* magazine from the 7-11. Back at home in my little apartment, I poured over the "Singers Wanted" section of *Music Connection*. I was itching to be in a band again. I was itching to start the life I had promised I would make for myself in Los Angeles.

"Lindsey Buckingham looking for his Stevie Nicks," an ad fished. I could picture the schmuck behind it, strumming his guitar with one hand, jerking off with the other. *Pass!*

"Singer wanted for goth/rock/synth/metal band about to take over the world," another read. "You preferably have a van or similar vehicle that we can tour in." Yeah... *Pass.*

Two ads garnered my interest: An all-girl band

named Blush needed a vocalist, and a songwriter was looking for a female singer to complete his punk band. I called both ads, and to my surprise, they both called me back. My first audition was for Blush. I knocked on an apartment door deep in the San Fernando Valley and was greeted by a militant woman with a bowl cut.

"Well, you're pretty. You'll do." She leaned out of her doorway, blonde hair skimming her eyelashes. "Sabrina." She looked me up and down before letting me in.

Sabrina's walls displayed various sizes of the same photo. A poster-size print overlooked her kitchen table; an 8x10 greeted you in the hallway. A 4x6 graced her coffee table. The photo was a good 10 years old, and in it, my militant lesbian host looked feminine and pretty, her blonde hair falling in soft curls around her shoulders. A brunette with a toothy grin stood beside her, arms outstretched as if mid-song.

"We almost had a record deal," she said, noting my interest. "Everyone fucks things up for me." She turned towards the photo, her tone accusing, bottom lip quivering. "Everyone."

I cleared my throat and Sabrina seemed to snap out of her posttraumatic episode.

"Did you practice the tape I sent you?" Sabrina had sent me a tape in the mail of three saccharine pop-punk songs. They were garbage. They reeked of the mall. I didn't care. I just wanted to be a part of SOMETHING.

"Yes, I loved them." I smiled at her. "Really unique stuff!"

Her lip softened. She grabbed an acoustic guitar and we sat down on her couch. She strummed her guitar as I sat back and watched, tapping my foot. Sabrina stopped abruptly and stared at me.

"This is where you siiiiiiiing," she said rolling her eyes.

"Sorry, I didn't know we were starting. I mean I didn't know—"

Her strumming interrupted me and my heart raced.

I counted four beats in my head and croaked out the first line. Sabrina stopped playing again.

"Okay, you're not going to work. Thanks for coming."

She stood up. I turned red.

"Well, can I try it again? I mean, I was kind of flustered, I just need to get into it."

"No, I need someone that's going to get it right away." She snapped her fingers together. "Like that! Thank you and goodbye."

I was dumbfounded. I'd never been so mortified in my life. She walked into the kitchen and began to scrub her dishes furiously as I saw myself out.

On the car ride home, I wished I'd punched Sabrina in the face. She hadn't even given me a chance! I wanted to turn around, knock on her door again, and tell her that her other band probably failed because she was an egotistical, psychotic bitch. I wanted to tell her that her music sucked. Instead, I put the tape back into my stereo and sang the first song out loud in my Probe. I sang it perfectly. Note for goddamn note.

I was still licking my wounds a week later as I hoofed it to Highland Park for my next audition. I drove through the avenues, genuine California gang land, and up into Mount Washington to a little house on a hillside. A short, doughy man glazed in a thin coat of sweat greeted me. He grinned like a Cheshire cat in heat, a thick caterpillar of a unibrow above his dark eyes.

"Welcome! Enter!" Mike was a songwriter in his forties. What he lacked in looks he had in riffs, and with a young thing like me on the microphone, perhaps he could finally get his due. We spent the afternoon going over his songs. He played his guitar and was patient when I was off-key and couldn't find the rhythm. Two days later, Mike called me and let me know I was a perfect fit. I had myself a band!

I spent many afternoons at his little house in the hills practicing our songs. Disapproving of my affinity for glam rock, Mike introduced me to California punk. The Dead Kennedys, Black Flag, and X became my new loves. I'd lie on his living room floor listening to the album *Los Angeles* over and over again.

When I wasn't indulging my newfound craving for intelligent punk, I was at the Rainbow in Hollywood. Growing up, I'd read about the Rainbow in heavy metal and hard rock magazines. My 11-year-old self had longed to tease my hair, put on a spandex dress and spiked-heel hooker boots, and slide into a red leather booth with a cup full of booze and some don't-give-a-fuck tattooed boy. The Rainbow was the Mecca for sleaze glam, right there on the Sunset Strip, an Aqua Net-scented wonderland where long-haired cock rockers flyered for their shows at the Coconut Teaser and the Troubadour. Every musician I'd ever fantasized about had hung out there, including the boys in Mötley Crüe, and of course, my Axl Rose.

I'd fallen in love with Axl Rose the first time I heard "Welcome to the Jungle." His high-pitched squeal made my preteen limbs quiver. I begged my stepfather to take me to Harmony House to buy the Guns N' Roses cassette tape, ripped open the packaging, and sucked in my breath as I beheld him. There he was, Axl Rose, staring back at me in all of his red-headed whiskey-swilling glory. I decided then and there I would marry him. He would be mine.

At 21, I was years late to the Sunset Strip party, but the glitter and glam still lingered within the heavy wooden walls of the Rainbow, where that phallic era refused to die. I set up camp there nightly with a tall blonde named Melissa that I'd met in the restroom. Axl Rose never did show up, but Melissa and I became best friends after she showed me who to buy coke from in the 'Bow's back stairwell. The faceless dealer would procure a baggie from the rafters in exchange for your twenty dollars. It had been almost eight months since I'd dropped my bullet on the floor of Cheetahs and the cocaine in my nostrils was like an old best friend.

Mike had just spent a small fortune on a week's

worth of recording for us at a studio in Burbank. We had an eight-song album and we'd just started to book shows. We played a couple small ones, and then we scored the Whiskey a Go Go. We had one week before the biggest gig I'd ever played.

"Why is your face breaking out like that?" Mike asked me one afternoon as I danced on his balcony to Fishbone.

"It's not!" *Shut up, fat fuck,* I thought to myself.

"Yes it is... And your attitude is shit lately. What're you doing?"

"NOTHING!"

"Are you doing coke? Speed? Come on, Autumn. You're too pretty for that. And your friends are bull-shit."

"*MY FRIENDS ARE BULLSHIT?*" I stopped dancing and marched over to where he sat eating his arugula salad in the sun. *Pompous ass.* "LEAVE ME ALONE!" I stuck a finger in his chest. "FUCK OFF!"

I put on my jacket and Mike followed me into his living room.

"Those people you call your friends just want you to be as miserable as they are."

"You're just jealous because you have no friends! I'm your only fucking friend!" I yelled back as I marched out to my car. Mike stared down from his window as I backed out of his long driveway, hitting his gnomes and rocks on the way down.

I didn't return his calls for the rest of the week. The day of our Whiskey show, he pounded on my door early in the morning. I'd been doing coke with

Melissa all week. I crept down to the door and opened it a crack.

"You look awful!" Mike said immediately.

"I have a cold." I glared at him through the crack.

"Wait here," he said as if I'd go anywhere. "I'll be back."

An hour later, Mike was back at my door with a bag of groceries from Trader Joe's. I let him in and laid on my couch, facing the other direction as he explained all the things he had bought. Throat Coat tea, honey, some healthy food, vitamins.

"Autumn! Are you listening? We have a show tonight and I need you to be well... I can help you make this stuff."

"I'm not going tonight."

"*What?* Are you fucking serious?"

"I don't want to."

Mike looked down at me curled up in the fetal position. I gazed back at him. I wanted to tell him the truth: I was afraid of being judged. I was afraid of success. It was easier to lie there on the sofa. It was easier to choose the drugs over a chance at anything.

"Stupid kid. You could be anything you want." He put the bag of groceries down by the door and left. It was the last time I would ever see him.

15.

SIX FOOT, REVOLVING VAGINAS

THE SIGN OUT FRONT OF THE CENTURY advertised "Live Nude Nudes" in orange and red psychedelic lettering. *Well, live nude girls are better than dead nude girls,* I thought to myself as I parked my car. It seemed like a classy enough place.

A ponytailed doorman with one eye fused shut and a clip-on bow tie showed me around my new place of employment.

"We used to be a disco in the seventies," he said, voice booming like a radio announcer's. "Want to see something really special?"

I followed him to the back of the bar where he pushed open a door to reveal the bones of a bowling alley that used to run on the weekends there. He put one finger to his chapped lips and winked at me with his good eye. I giggled.

Even in the middle of the day the main floor of the Century Lounge was bustling. Businessmen waiting for flights home to their nagging wives lined the stage, wagging their tongues, while strippers in day-glow pink and yellow slingshot bikinis competed for their dollars.

"And here's where the magic happens," said my tour guide, motioning towards a row of dance booths with token machines attached. I'd never seen anything like it. You drop in a coin and *voila!* The booth would light up and a naked girl of your choice would cavort about in front of you. There were also private booths in different areas of the bar where they offered up nude lap dances. The thought of rubbing my bare vagina against a stranger's dirty blue jeans on a pleather couch in the middle of the afternoon wasn't exactly my idea of a good time, but dances at the Century were 40 bucks a pop. After struggling to make a decent income in Los Angeles' topless bars, I knew that this job would add up fast.

I eagerly signed my paperwork and started my shift.

The stage itself was the most fascinating thing about the Century Lounge. Two gigantic screens hung from the ceiling on both sides and a clear panel in the center of it housed an upwards-facing camera with the sole purpose of capturing beaver shots. All Century girls were required to spread their legs over the glass for at least fifteen long seconds so that a smug-looking cameraman in a booth across from the stage could get a solid money shot. When he had his shot, he would project pure, unadulterated vagina onto both big screens where it would circle at varying speeds.

Before my first set, I mentally and physically prepared myself for my girl's first big-screen show. After looking around to make sure I was alone, I bent over a backstage mirror and spread myself apart. No stray pieces of toilet paper, no tampon strings. I'd even taken extra care shaving that day and my pubic hair formed a neat little 'stache that I was quite proud of.

Hell, I even had a brand new name. "And right now we have Madeleine! It's Madeleine's first day here at the Century, make her feel welcome!" the DJ announced as I parted the thick velvet curtain that separated the dressing area from the main stage. I beamed at the crowd. It was always good to be under the hot red lights of a new place.

Adrenaline raced through my veins. Everyone always ogled the new girl: managers, bartenders, regulars, and especially the other strippers. They all watched with sharp eyes and tongues, knowing no one holds power like a fresh, new girl. Dollar bills littered my stage. The second song was half over before I remembered that I should be panty-less. I peeled off my underwear and slung-shot them across the stage to join my bikini top.

Out of the corner of my eye I saw the manager next to Chris the cameraman, arms folded in the booth. Chris gave me a solemn nod. It was my time to head over to the camera. *Ugh.* Slowly, I spread my legs over the clear plexiglass and looked up at the video screen for the big reveal.

I quickly learned that even the most well-groomed vaginas became horror shows when enlarged to big screen proportions.

The men, however, seemed drawn to six-foot revolving vaginas. As soon as I got off stage I had dances waiting for me. My first customer wore track pants. Men who wore track pants to strip clubs usually meant business. We went to one of the private booths and I popped a token in. Our booth lit up, I took my panties off, and I hopped down on his lap. His hands immediately clutched at my breasts.

"Hey, watch it," I said, brushing away his eager fingers.

"You're a tough one. All the other girls let me touch." He smirked as he spoke.

"I'm not 'all the other girls.'"

"Well, you should ask your coworkers about how things are done around here."

I rolled my eyes, turned my back to him, and began to grind on him. He dug his hands into my thighs and pumped back in hard, fast thrusts.

"I'm doing the dancing here," I said, jumping off of his lap. "Relax."

"Okay, sorry. Just keep going," he whined.

I sat down on him again and grazed my ass cheeks against his swollen member slowly, sensually. He moaned and clutched at my legs a second time, pumping away. I tried to stand and he gripped me tighter, then collapsed against my back as quickly as he began.

"Unghhhhhh," he whimpered, shuddering.

I felt a warm wetness on the back of my ass.

"Did you fucking come on me?" I jumped off of his lap, touching the sticky dampness that had seeped from his track pants onto my bare skin.

"You think I can get off in one dance? Don't flatter yourself, honey," he said, standing up as his cock bulged around a telltale wet spot. He counted out four ten-dollar bills for me. No tip. I shoved past him, heading back to the dressing room, where I doused my ass with rubbing alcohol.

Welcome to Hollywood, I thought to myself. I sniffed a line of coke from my bullet.

16.

PRETTY GIRLS DO UGLY THINGS

STRIPPERS, WELL... THEY WERE THE SAME everywhere: An army of wise women with frosted makeup and fake hair who had mastered a quicker route to a man's wallet than dating or marriage. Even the youngest ones quickly became machines, their eyes blank as they petitioned the Century Lounge-goers for dances. The men that sipped juice at the nude bars in Los Angeles, however, were light years away from the red-blooded factory workers whose laps I'd graced back home. Those men had been fairly vanilla in their tastes, just looking for an escape from their Midwestern wives, but this crowd had quirks and fetishes.

The "sniffer" would come in and see me a couple of times a week. We'd make our way to a booth and I'd sit on his lap and hold up my arm while he breathed in the scent from my armpits for a whole two songs. One of my other clients owned a popular hilltop restaurant, and when he wasn't catering to high society, he liked me to place the six-inch heel of my stripper shoe on his cock and press down hard. The louder he moaned the more pressure I'd apply. I imagined his cock snapping in half under my acrylic heel. Yet another customer liked to put a dog collar on and bark when I danced with him. The exit from a booth after he had been howling and yapping like a Beagle for a half hour was embarrassing, but the fifty-dollars-a-song made it bearable.

Some of the customers' whims I couldn't bring myself to fulfill. At the beginning of one of my shifts, a man flagged me down for a dance. We made our way back to a booth. I stripped off my costume and began to play with my tits.

"Can you put your ass in my face?" he asked.

I took off my heels and stood on the leather arm-rests of the couch, shaking my butt against his nose. He groaned with pleasure.

"I'll pay you extra if you go take a shit and don't wipe," he said, licking his lips.

"What?" I turned around to face him, wrinkling my nose.

"You know... I want to smell your shit. Please? I'll tip you really well!"

"I'll pass," I said.

As different as my customers' tastes were, they all had a common bond: They were looking for something they'd lost long ago. They were looking for someone to make them feel like men again, if only in three-minute-long increments set to Foghat's "Slow-ride." When the wives pushed them away or started treating them like less-than-ordinary men, they came to me to fill the void. I asked them how their day was when their wives forgot to ask or had stopped caring. I laughed at their jokes, played with their hair, feigned fascination at their mundane traits, cooed over their computer job—and was handsomely rewarded for it.

Besides cold hard cash, I had amassed a Rolodex full of services men could render for me if need be: a mechanic, a guy to fix the locks, a guy to get the dent out of my car where I had rubbed it against a pole high on coke, a tile guy, a fisherman that brought me fresh Mahi Mahi steaks, a pet store owner that gave me a vapid little dog, the DMV guy that let me cut in line.

In the time I'd been a dancer, I had learned the power of a smile to someone who was nagged at home or stuck in a shit job, the power of a simple touch on a stranger's hand or cheek. If I could remember their name the second time they came in, even better. Fantasy or not, the renewed faith in themselves as men that they took home was priceless to them.

My shifts at the Century began at 7 p.m. and ended at 4 in the morning. At the end of my shift, I'd head to the Taco Bell down the street for a quesadilla, or to Jerry's Deli for soup with one of the other girls. I'd pull up to my Burbank apartment as the sun was rising and do a line or two of cocaine, watching the world wake up from my window as I counted and faced my piles of money. I'd sleep most of the day away, wake up to another line of coke, then head to the mall to spend other peoples' husband's and father's money on whatever I desired at the moment: designer jeans, makeup, shoes, a set of DVDs that would teach me Spanish that I would never open. One day I bought a parrot just because I had 900 dollars in my pocket. I gave it away to a bird sanctuary a week later because it bored me. Everything had started to bore me. How was it that the men seemed so full after they left, and though they filled my pockets, they left me feeling so empty?

I was losing track of the days. . . losing focus.

17.

THE ACTUARY

I MET RICHARD AFTER I'D BEEN AT THE CEN-tury for three months. He slouched in his thin athletic shorts and tattered NRA t-shirt, his lower lip and belly jutting out to match his slouching walk. Richard was Erica's regular. Erica was a fading flower who wore a synthetic blonde wig while she worked at the Century in a failed attempt to hide her identity. She'd prostituted up in San Fran during the big dot-com boom and saved enough money to buy herself a bakery in Los Angeles. Her business had gone under in less than a year and she'd started stripping to pick up the pieces. She bounced around like a 20-year-old, but her face and ass had the weariness of a woman in her 40s who'd lost it all and had no chance of regaining it.

All Richard had lost, on that particular Thursday afternoon, were his car keys.

I overheard him at the bar, asking if anyone had turned them in.

"These keys?" I asked, twirling a set on my finger.

I'd found them in a lap dance booth just moments before.

"Yes!" Richard beamed at me. "How about a dance, as a reward for finding them for me?"

"Sure," I said, leading him to a corner booth. I popped my token in, and our red light came on. I cautiously rubbed my knee between his legs. Heavyset guys were always hard to dance for. You spent more time riding on their bellies than their cocks. I decided conversation would work better on this one.

"What do you do?" I asked.

"I'm an actuary," he said

"What's that?" I turned to shake my ass in his face.

"I'm a risk assessor."

"Sounds math-y," I laughed. "I'm a musician."

"Well, there's math in music," he said.

"I guess that's why I'm still no good at the violin after 20 years of playing it," I teased.

"Beautiful and you play the violin?" His loose lower lip curved upward as his meaty hands caressed my back. "How come I never noticed you before?"

From that evening on, Richard only came to the Century Lounge to see me. Erica would glare at me in her space-stripper-from-Mars costume when he'd arrive promptly at 7 p.m. for my shift, bearing my dinner: a tuna fish sandwich from Subway and a peach milkshake from Mello Burger. I was half afraid she'd shiv me in the parking lot after work.

Richard and I would eat together and talk before heading to our favorite booth. I knew all about his wife who bored him and wanted to take more college courses instead of getting a job, his son who was going through an awkward phase and called "Snacks" by his classmates, his mother who had recently died, and his father who was coping with it. In turn, I told Richard my dreams: I wanted to be an actress and a real musician. I knew I could do it. So many others less worthy were out there doing it! Richard agreed. He would sit on my stage as I danced to The Police, eyes in a dreamlike trance.

"Awhoooooooo!" he would howl, head thrown back as I pulled my panties around my thighs.

I had to share some of my money with the club and Richard didn't think that was right. He suggested me giving him lap dances in a hotel room instead.

"I'm not going to have sex with you," I said, arms folded.

"I didn't ask you to," Richard pouted.

A week later I met him at a Motel 6 in the San Fernando Valley. He was on the bed waiting for me in his knit shorts, my tuna fish sandwich and peach shake sitting on the bedside table. Richard unwrapped my sandwich for me, grinned, and rubbed his hands together as I took my first bite. He loved to watch me eat, as if I was a stray, malnourished puppy he had found on the street. I chewed in silence. The lights of the Motel 6 cast a stark reality over the situation.

"Time to get to work," Richard said as soon as I'd had my fill. He switched on a boom box he had brought with him.

I stripped off my clothes as he lay across the bed,

his thick, tree-trunk legs hanging off the edge, feet enclosed in old, worn socks. His legs were almost purple near the calves. I'd never noticed in the dark at the club. I climbed onto the bed and straddled his belly. My thigh grazed his fleshy stomach where his t-shirt rode up on him. He closed his eyes as I rubbed my naked body against his clothing. My stomach gurgled. Two hours was going to seem like an eternity without the backdrop of a loud strip club to keep me going.

"Let me just hold you," Richard said after a while, so I turned my back to him and he spooned me from behind. His breath was heavy. He exhaled as if he hadn't held a woman in decades. I was stiff. My stomach turned at his touch. I imagined myself anywhere but there in that room with his breath in my hair. When it was time to go, Richard folded 500 dollars in my hand.

Back at home that night, I sat on my window ledge doing lines of coke by myself. The sirens wailed outside my apartment. I knew I'd be back to Motel 6. I didn't want to but it was too easy and I was tired.

At the end of a year of tuna fish sandwiches, peach smoothies and lap dances, I had accumulated over 60,000 dollars from Richard—an impressive amount of cash from a man whose job was to deal with the financial impact of risk and uncertainty.

18.

HIGH BEAMS AND HEARTACHES

IMPLANTS WERE A COMMON ACQUISITION in Los Angeles and I decided I would need some, too. An agent I'd met at the Century set me up with a commercial audition that I inexplicably booked, and one day on set earned me a $6,000 check, which was roughly the cost of a set of fake knockers. I wanted C cups, round and high. I chose Dr. Linder to give them to me because I'd seen his work at many strip clubs, most impressively on a stripper named Gypsy, who was probably 50 but had the tits of a 19-year-old.

"You see how this one is a little tubular," Dr. Linder said, poking at my meager breasts. "We're going to get you some big C cups and you're going to look great."

I put down a deposit of $3,000, set a surgery date, and went back in the following week for my blood work—a series of tests to make sure that I was healthy enough for the surgery. A couple of days later, a nurse called from the clinic.

"Miss Franklin?"

"Yes?"

"Are you aware that you're pregnant? We're going to have to cancel your surgery."

I was silent for a moment. "That's impossible."

"I'm sorry," she said.

I hung up the phone and sat on the edge of my bed with my head in my hands.

That night at work, as I wandered the floor looking for lap dances, a man called me over and grazed my stomach with his hand. I drew back in absolute horror. The thought of giving a lap dance with a tiny human growing inside me was revolting. I wanted it out immediately. I didn't want to be a mother. I didn't want to be stretched beyond repair or have my breasts and dreams sucked dry. I didn't want the responsibility of taking care of another life. And I wanted that fucking boob job.

I had to call Drew.

I'd met Drew when I was 23 years old. He was forty, owned a porn production company, and had been in a glam rock band that I'd swooned over when I was in junior high. I worked with a stripper named Kat who happened to be dating his best friend and business partner. I'd been insanely jealous of Kat since the first time I'd laid eyes on her. She brought me to a party they were having at their studio, and before I knew better, I'd swallowed a hit of ecstasy.

"She took the whole thing?" Drew asked, eyes wide.

"Yeah, what's the big deal?" Kat rolled her seafoam eyes.

"It was cut with heroin, that's the big deal! You know that! It's way too strong," he said as she giggled. "My god, you're a cunt, Kat."

A half hour later I heard voices from every corner of the room yelling at me. They weaved in and out of my brain as Kat smiled and waved, sticking out her long, pink tongue at me. The next morning I woke up in Drew's bed, trying to remember the night before: There had been dancing. There was a trip to CVS for giant cellophane Easter rabbit balloons. And there must have been lots of sex with Drew.

He turned over to look at me with the greenest eyes I'd ever seen.

"You fuck so good for a girl your age," he said, kissing me on the nose. "Where did you learn that?"

I shrugged my shoulders and snuggled up against him.

I started to see Drew a few times a week for dinner and, of course, sex. We had incredible chemistry in bed and zero in conversation. I'd sit across from him at a table while he ate his food and said nothing to me. I tried to tell him about my days —about an audition or the band that I was working with when I wasn't dancing topless somewhere. His facial expression sometimes feigned interest but he was never really listening.

After the first night we were together, he never turned over to face me as we slept. I never felt him curve his body around mine. After we fucked, he slept flat on his back. He'd lay so flat and so still that I was afraid to breathe because I thought I'd wake him.

Sometimes I watched him silently. I wanted so badly for him to love me, to be proud of me, or be affected by me at all.

I knew this news would affect him but I wasn't sure how. That night, I sat with my phone in my hand, dreading the call I had to make.

"Hello?" he answered groggily.

"Hi."

"It's late," he said.

"I know. I'm sorry. I hope it's okay that I called, it's just that..." I began to cry. He surely wouldn't love me after this conversation. "I'm pregnant," I said.

"Are you sure?

"Positive."

The other end of the phone was silent.

"Let's go have dinner tomorrow," he finally said after a long exhale.

The next evening I drove over to Drew's and picked him up. We didn't speak in the car, and we didn't speak as we slid into the leather booth at Gladstone's.

"You know, I don't know if I'm ready to be a father," he finally blurted out. I looked at the 40-year-old man in front of me, his eyes green gems nestled in his crow's feet.

"It's okay. I'll get rid of it."

"Okay. I'll pay for it."

We ate our fish in sheepish guilt.

I was able to schedule an abortion for two days later so that I could keep my appointment for breast implants with Dr. Linder. Drew picked me up and took me to a woman's clinic in Burbank. They asked for payment first, but he'd conveniently forgotten his credit cards at home, so I plunked down my own Visa card and a pretty nurse took me in the back.

"How are you?" She flashed her veneers at me.

I wanted to punch her. *How did she think I was?* I took off my clothing and covered myself with a paper hospital robe. The room was freezing. I lay down on a medical table and placed my feet in the forceps. A grey-whiskered doctor entered the room and stretched medical gloves over his long fingers, clicking his tongue at me. I half-wondered if he would sterilize me while he was down there. He brought out a needle full of anesthesia, the longest I'd ever seen, long enough to poke into my cervix.

"This is going to hurt, " he said.

I screamed as he inserted the needle. The nurse squeezed my hand as tears rolled down my cheeks. The anesthesia was only to numb me to a bearable point. I would be awake for the rest of the procedure. I tried to remain still as the doctor stretched my cervix and went to work with the aspirator. My stomach cramped and I howled.

"Your hair is so long." The nurse clutched my hand, trying to calm me. "But you've got split ends, you should cut it a little."

I wanted to spit in her face. I had a vacuum in my vagina and she was talking about my split ends.

The process couldn't have taken more than fifteen minutes but it felt like hours had gone by. When it was done they left me to lie on the cold metal table

by myself. Drew came back to see me after a few minutes.

"Are you done?" he asked.

"I think so." I stared up at the ceiling.

"Let's get out of here, then." He propped me up.

"I think I'm supposed to sit here and—"

"Oh, you're fine, you're a tough chick." He helped
me off the table and into my clothes and we walked
out to the waiting room.

"Sir! Where are you taking her?" The nurse caught
us as we approached the door.

"She's done, she wants to leave," Drew snapped
back.

The nurse blocked our exit. "She has instructions
and meds to take, she could get an infection!"

The doctor came into the waiting room, furious.
He shook his head as he handed me a prescription for
antibiotics and instructions and then we were off in
Drew's Jeep.

Drew dropped me off at home, saying he had to
get back to work. He told me he'd come see me later
but he didn't. He didn't answer my phone calls either.

Two weeks later I had my breast surgery. My implants were put under the muscle because I had
such a tiny frame. I knew it would be painful, but
when the initial anesthesia and medication wore off,
the pain was almost unbearable. I felt as if I'd been
beaten head-to-toe with a baseball bat.

The pain all over my body was joined by the ache
in my heart. I was in bed for two weeks. Drew didn't
call. My mother came to take care of me for a few days,

and then Patrick, a guy that I'd been dating before I met Drew, took over. He cooked for me, cleaned for me, bathed me, and drove me to my doctor's appointments. At night he propped me up and slept against me so that I would stay asleep in the proper position.

"I just want to see you smile again. Does it really hurt that bad?" Patrick asked, tousling my hair. He was a good guy, and I wished that I could love him, but I just couldn't.

"Yes. Worse than anything." I stared at the ceiling, imagining Patrick's waxy face in a casket, surrounded by Begonias.

After I was healed-up enough to drive, I went to visit Drew at his office. I needed to see him. His receptionist paled when she saw me come in.

"Drew's not here," she said like a pre-recorded message.

"I know he is. I saw his car out front."

"I'm sorry, but he's very busy."

My heart beat harder in my chest as I reddened. "Well, you tell him that I came by to get my five hundred dollars for my fucking abortion." The office grew still and silent. Someone cleared their throat nervously. "And you can tell him that I'll be back here every day until I get it!"

I sat in my car for a while, feeling lightheaded and staring at the world outside. The sun was bright and silhouetted the California mountains. I laughed. Somehow I'd found so much ugliness in such a beautiful place. I released the wail that I'd been holding in for six weeks. I cried for dead fetuses, for so many levels of pain, for the two weeks spent in bed. I banged my cowboy boot against the front window of my Probe until it cracked. I wanted my mother, and I wanted to go home.

I'd been so stupid. Why hadn't I offed him when I had the chance? Think fast, think fast... Pneumonia. It was all the drugs. He was so unhealthy. He caught pneumonia and just couldn't shake it. Everyone agreed that it was a horrible, horrible situation. He looked like shit at his funeral. He was grey, and the only good part of him, those gorgeous green eyes, were shut tight to the world. I made a quick appearance. I left black roses for him. Two.

Three days later, there was a check stuffed in my mailbox. I spent Drew's five hundred dollars on a ticket to Detroit. A week later I found myself on a plane, arms crossed protectively around my new breasts, cocaine baggie hidden in the lining of my underwear, antibiotics for my two surgeries in my pocket, and Incubus's "Wish You Were Here" ringing in my ears through my headphones.

13.

DOWN THE RABBIT HOLE

FOUR YEARS AFTER MY PILGRIMAGE TO Los Angeles, my self-fulfilling prophecy became reality. I had big fake breasts and was up for a new Playboy TV show. The concept was fairly simple: three anchorwomen would strip down to nothing while they reported the daily news.

The day of my audition, I fidgeted in the waiting room of the Playboy offices, tearing off bits of paper from my script until all I had left in my palm was clammy pulp. I was already regretting my choice to wear my freshly-blonde hair curly, and wished that I had sprung for a new bra and panty set. Would they notice my bruised stripper knees? I shouldn't have eaten breakfast, either. My stomach lurched and I briefly considered heading to the bathroom for a quick purge so that it'd look flatter.

A perfect brunette sat across from me, completely unaffected by what lay ahead of her, French-manicured fingers flipping the pages of a *Playboy* magazine on the coffee table in front of us.

"I'm in this one!" she cooed in my general direction.

"I'm not," I said.

"Ashley! Girlfriend!" A blonde with milky skin flitted into the room and made a beeline for the brunette. "I knew you'd be here. We book everything together!" The brunette stood up and squeaked back at the blonde, their bodies combined into one perfect sex bomb, Louis Vuitton bags clinking cheers. I rolled my eyes and scraped at the acne scab on my chin.

"Autumn?" The casting assistant came out, calling my name off his clipboard.

"That's me." I stood up, adjusted my skirt, awkwardly gathered up my belongings, and followed him to the casting room. I was greeted by the producer and director, both of whom looked disgruntled and tired. Before the sight of those two, I hadn't thought that men could tire of an endless stream of girls taking off their clothes all day long.

"Hi, I'm Autumn," I said, turning on as much sunshine as I could muster.

"Hello, Autumn!" They looked me up and down. No matter how many auditions I went on, having someone scrutinize me head to toe for television worthiness would never get more comfortable. I felt my skin bloat under their gaze, pimples head before their eyes. I was perpetually a fat 13-year-old.

"Beautiful girl! Let me give you some notes before you read for us. We need some personality here. No one is coming here and putting life into this script. We want smiles, excitement... This is the news, but this is Playboy, got it?"

"I think so!" I was sweating.

"Great! Sorry we don't have a prompter for you today, you can read off this board." An assistant flipped a video camera on while another held up a poster with the script handwritten in giant letters. I shifted my weight from heel to heel, cleared my throat, and smiled my biggest soft-core porn smile.

"Hi, I'm Autumn Franklin, and you are watching Playboy TV's Weekend Flash. Real news, real people... Real naked. In today's episode..." The script came out of my mouth verbatim, as if I had been possessed.

"Start taking your clothes off," the director whispered loudly. I had almost forgotten about that part.

As I spoke, I slowly unbuttoned my shirt, took it off, and then hung it over my shoulder for a moment before tossing it to the ground. I wriggled out of my skirt and gave it a playful kick to the side when it hit the floor. I decided to take off my panties before my bra, something I was sure the competition wouldn't have thought of. Thumbs hooked around the sides of my lace panties, I tugged them left and right for a moment, then pulled them off in a slight profile pose. Kicking out one hip, I finally unhooked my bra and landed in a saucy hands-on-hip pose.

"Thanks for watching, make sure you tune in tomorrow!" I finished, throwing in a wink for the camera.

"Yes, a girl that can read. You were a little fast but it had flavor," the director beamed. "Thank you for coming in!"

I put my clothes back on and shook their hands. They were friendly and I felt confident. Apparently, I hadn't had fake tits long enough to cloud the part of your brain that could take simple direction and think and read. I stole one more look at the doe-eyed, bobble-headed bitches in the waiting room on my way out and tried to forget that I had just gone on the biggest audition of my life. I didn't really have delusions about booking the job did I? After all, it was Playboy. All the brains in the world couldn't beat out blonde hair and a silicone smile. Or could they?

Weeks passed. I had given up on the job altogether when I got the call.

"Autumn, are you sitting down?" Gloria, a portly manager that had scouted me at the Beverly Hills mall, chortled into the phone. She always sounded like she was out of breath or choking on a sandwich. I was lying down with a migraine. I had been on a coke bender for a week with a bearded boy named Darryl. My head throbbed as I sat up in bed.

"You got the job. You are Playboy TV's new entertainment reporter! They're going to pay you $100,000 a year. ONE HUNDRED THOUSAND DOLLARS, AUTUMN! They're faxing over contracts this week."

I was speechless. I looked at the boy next to me, sleeping in his sweat, and then looked at the mirror adjacent to my bed. Me? I had beat out hundreds of nubile minxes to become Playboy TV's naked entertainment news anchor?

"Holy shit, Gloria!"

"You're my little star, Autumn!!"

Later that week, I had a meet and greet with my two costars, a ditzy weather girl and the hard news anchorwoman. We lunched with the producer, who was giddy over the concept for his new show. We were all going to be stars.

Katrina, the hard news girl, grabbed my hand and looked at me, brushing the hair out of my eyes. "You are so pretty," she said. I shrugged my shoulders. "Did you hear me?" She cupped my chin and looked me in the eye. "You are stunning, one of the prettiest people I've ever seen."

I looked down. I didn't feel particularly pretty. "Thank you," I mumbled.

Playboy built us a real newsroom set. Walking out onto our sound stage, you could've been at CNN, ET, EXTRA... Except for the fact that we stripped down to nothing while we reported. The first few weeks on set were a whirlwind. We had press from all over the world dropping by to speak with us, and the crew was busy working out studio bugs. Once the excitement started to wear off, everyone was on edge. Our show was expensive to make. Our salaries were too high. The studio had gone over budget.

"This movie makes *Dances with Wolfs* look like *Slaughterhouse Five.*" I was on my new movie segment late one Friday when the cameras stopped rolling and a voice came over the speakers in the control room.

"It's wolves, not wolfs, do it again." The producer's voice was like the voice of god, pointing an angry invisible finger at me.

"That's what I said."

"No, you said 'woof,' like a goddamn dog barking. It's *wolves.*"

The camera fired up once more. We didn't do edits, so I would have to do my whole segment over again. I put my clothes back on and re-started the script. It was perfect until the sentence happened again.

"This movie makes *Dances with Wolfs...* fuck!" I wanted to cry. "I'm sorry, I'm sorry..."

"BACK THE FUCKING PROMPTER UP!" the producer screamed through the speaker.

I was shaking. On my third attempt, I tripped up the first part of the script.

"BACK IT UP!"

I tried to relax myself. I had to do it; I had to get through one complete take.

"And this movie makes *Dances with Wuulves* look like *Slaughterhouse Five.* I'm Autumn, see you next week!" The studio was silent as we waited for the producer's approval to move on. I felt like I was suffocating under the lights.

"That was passable. We've got to move on people, we are a fucking half hour behind schedule!"

I couldn't breathe. Woof, wolf, did it really matter?

The next day I was sent to a vocal coach, courtesy of the Bunny, to rid me of my intolerable Michigander accent and my inability to properly address Mr. Canis Lupus. I drove out to the depths of the San Fernando Valley where a middle-aged man with three first names and breath like stale orange juice led me to a guest house where he taught lessons in vocal awareness to budding stars. We sat down face to face.

"What you have to do is unlock your voice," he said, a crêpe-like dirge rising from his throat. An ominous click came from the depths of it, like he needed a goddamn drink of water. I'd had a math tutor with the same impediment. It made me want to stab him in the neck with my pencil for an hour straight each Tuesday. I failed algebra that year.

"Something that happened to you is holding back your voice, you have to address that to make it strong."

I drifted away. *I was in the third grade; we had a talent show at school. My friends and I decided to do Whitney Houston's "Greatest Love of All." We met after school three days a week at June Cole's house so that her mother could coach us, a woman who'd never gotten over leaving her theater days in New York City for a man that later divorced her and left her with two daughters in a crappy Southfield apartment.*

"Sing like the strong black woman you are, Autumn! Be the strong black woman!" Her eyes bugged and her upper lip sweated as she directed me, big hips swaying.

"Do you want to go over your script?"

"What?"

"Your script, do you want to go over it?"

"Oh, yeah..." I shuffled the papers in my hands.

"Why don't you stand up and read it."

The man with three first names crossed his legs as I stood in front of him.

"And in other entertainment news, the Latin Grammys..."

"Slow down, slow down..."

"And in other... entertainment news... the Latin Grammys..."

Three names rubbed his jaw line with a hairy hand.

"You know, this is just a thought, but would it help you to take your clothes off and maybe do it topless like you do on the show?"

I looked up from my paper and scowled at him.

"Just a thought," he said.

The next day of shooting, I read my lines off the teleprompter slowly and accurately.

"Where's the personality, Autumn?" the voice of god spoke from the control room.

I rolled my eyes. Katrina glared at me from her corner of the set. Initially, my costars and I had gotten along swimmingly. The Bunny was funneling all sorts of money into our TV show and plastering our faces all over *Playboy* Magazine. We had hair and makeup and wardrobe and fancy catering. We had dressing rooms emblazoned with our names. We three were the Charlie's Angels of the news world. And we only had to work one day a week, to boot. But women made fickle friends and our easy camaraderie turned to chemical warfare. The makeup room was ground zero. Small, cutting remarks flicked against my skin like rubber bands when I entered. *Did you gain weight? Man, you look tired! You think about Botox yet?*

A triple shot vanilla latte and a few lines of cocaine were necessary to prepare myself for the Friday ahead of me. The combination didn't bode well for my predisposition to motor-mouthing the weekend report off the teleprompter. The director was beside himself, stopping me often and enthusiastically, while the other girls snickered, basking in my dejection. The makeup girl tried her best to cover up my acne and the dark circles that had made a permanent home on my face. The stress, coke, and sleepless nights were eating me from the inside out. But when the reviews came in, much to the dismay of the producer, the director, and Queen Katrina, people adored me. I was not your typical Playboy girl. I was curvy and brown and it had garnered me diehard fans.

My curves became Katrina 's new target. One morning I arrived on set starving. Kraft service was just setting up but they had a plate of small taquitos out for the crew. Not my usual breakfast choice, but I knew I wouldn't be able to read off the teleprompter without eating something. I grabbed one and took it to set with me as Katrina watched from a distance.

We'd just begun filming when suddenly she doubled over, clutching her stomach.

"What's that smell?" She asked. "Oh my god, that smell!" She covered her mouth with a tiny hand, puffing out her cheeks. "I'm going to throw up! I can't stand the smell."

The PA desperately looked around for the source of the smell that was upsetting the talent.

"I can't find anything," he said, shrugging his shoulders.

Katrina's tiny body began to heave. She was thin, but years of excessive exercise and bulimia made her skin hang off her bones.

"What's the problem down there?" the director demanded from the sound room down the hall.

"I think it's Autumn's taquitos. She has a taquito out here and it just smells so bad, I can't read my lines," she whined, uncovering her nose and mouth just long enough to place the blame on me for fouling the place up.

My face grew hot; my skin tingled and begged me to react. I wanted to march over to her slowly, calmly. "I'm sorry, Katrina, I should be more sensitive to the fact that you have such a weak stomach," I'd say. Then I would take off my shoe, my six-inch clear acrylic heel, and slam it into her eyeball. Or I could grab her by her ponytail, force her veneers against the curb of our set, and stomp on the back of her skull. Of course, I couldn't *really* do any of those things. Instead, I did a Predator march over to my taquitos, picked one up, and threw it directly at her face. Her mouth pursed like a garage sale doll's but she didn't speak. No one spoke. The PA bent over to pick up the stray taquito. I stared back at her before turning on my heel and marching back to my dressing room.

I closed the door behind me and sat in the dark. How was it that I was doing something that I had always dreamed of and it fucking sucked?

I'd just thrown a taquito at someone.

I was miserable.

20.

PORCELAIN SMILES

"WHAT IS THIS?" I STORMED OUT OF MY dressing room, thrusting a foot-long fuck toy at the producer of our show.

He grinned back at me. "THAT," he said, "is the Oscillator. And YOU are going to pretend that you used it last night, absofuckinglutely loved it, and review it on one of your segments today."

"But I didn't."

"Well, they're giving us money, so your job is to say you did."

"They're giving the show money, not me. I'm not doing it. My job is to report the news, not review sex toys." I could smell Katrina's perfume. I knew she was listening at the door. "I don't even fucking use dildos!"

"So, now you're refusing to do your job?" The producer put his hands on his hips, challenging me with his eyes.

"No, I'm refusing to do something that's not in my job description. It doesn't say 'Oscillator tester' in my goddamn job description."

"You watch your mouth!" He pointed a fat finger at me, turned, and slammed my dressing room door.

"Fucking prick!" I yelled after him, kicking the door for emphasis. I held the Oscillator with a death grip in my hand before throwing it against the wall. It snapped in two pieces.

"Made in FUCKING China crap!" I screamed as I kicked at the pieces. I hadn't even been to hair and makeup yet and my day was ruined. I needed to relax. I laid out two lines of coke on my dressing room table and snorted them both back. I wasn't going to be pushed around anymore by a bunch of people who behaved like they were putting on a high school play rather than a hit TV show. I wasn't their fucking puppet. If I wanted to go home and oscillate my clit until it was mincemeat that was my business, but I wasn't going to talk about it so a corporation could make more money.

I ate lunch with the sound guys that day and saved my smiles for the camera. I only had to work one long day each week. One day of bickering with Katrina and the producer. My contract prohibited me from working other jobs and that left me with six idle days that I had nothing to fill with but drugs and shopping. My paycheck was hefty but boredom ran me dry. I started to miss stripping. I missed the one-on-one contact with people. I missed the stage. I found a tiny club in the valley where I was sure no one would recognize me and went back to work a couple days a week.

A short time later, I had an assignment to interview a celebrity. I arrived at the Playboy offices for
hair and makeup and was instead ushered into my
producer's office where two men in black suits sat
with him with my contract in hand.

"Sit down, Autumn," my producer said, his eyes
little glimmering slits. He folded and unfolded his
hands like an excited child. "We received this in our
email yesterday."

I took the paper out of his hands and read it to
myself. "I seen Autumn Franklin working at a club in
the valley. I took her in the back and gang banged her
with my boys."

I laughed out loud at the absurdity of the email.
The rest of the room was still silent. "This is a joke,
right? I mean, you don't believe that?"

My producer smirked. The lawyers turned to the
page in my contract that prohibited me from working
other jobs. My face grew hot and their words blended
together incoherently, but I could understand that I
was being fired. Two security officers came in and escorted me out of the building as everyone came out of
their cubicles and watched.

The next day I woke up to a couriered copy of
my contract on my front porch, important clauses
highlighted. As quickly as it had begun, it was over.
One of my girlfriends from the strip club came over
for ice cream to help cheer me up, but as she licked at
her melting strawberry blonde ice cream cone, I saw
a strange satisfaction in her eyes. She was the only
one who knew that I wasn't supposed to be dancing

at the club. She knew my contract prohibited it. Her smile was porcelain. I wanted to break it in with my fist.

21.

OLD HELL PASO

EL PASO WAS A WASTELAND THAT I'D somehow managed to make it to twice in my life. Once on a business trip with Steven, the married, dysfunctional drummer I'd banged for a few months in high school, and then with Darryl Briggs.

An intoxicatingly interesting juxtaposition of human flesh had turned me on to the man the instant my fawn skin brushed against his beastly arm at a rock show. At six-foot-four-inches tall, he had a voice with the cadence of Mississippi country molasses. His arms were cuffed by thick leather straps and his camouflage shorts were so old that he'd taped them up where holes had worn through in the back. His beard was long and braided in two ropes with silver skulls tied to their frayed ends. Darryl was a heavy metal singer. His father, Darryl Senior, had managed to make it big enough as a country singer to play the Grand Ol' Opry, only to jump in front of a big rig after his show when Darryl Jr.'s mother rejected him despite his accomplishment. At least that's what

Darryl Jr. had to say about it.

Though he had a band back in El Paso, Darryl had been in Los Angeles drying out for a couple years. I found it hard to believe that anyone would come to LA for that reason, but Darryl swore it was so. Our first few months of dating, however, had been high-lighted by just the opposite: drug binges, public fights, jumping out of running cars, and glass bottles to the back of the head. We decided it was love, and when his old band invited him back to El Paso to play a show with Judas Priest, I would join him.

Darryl thought it was a stellar chance for me to see him in his true element—underneath the hot lights of a big stage. He made the trip out a few days before me on the El Paso Express, a bus line that catered to those in need of a cheap, straight shot from Los Angeles to the seedy city that glared at Juarez, Mexico through barbed wire fences.

I dropped Darryl off at the station and watched as he waded through a sea of tiny brown people. He'd be sweating out toxins on that bus for two days to a broken English soundtrack. I had decided I'd fly out a few days later. I still had some Playboy money left. Playboy money could buy me a proper plane ticket. Fuck the El Paso Express.

When Darryl and his band mates picked me up at the airport, I could tell he'd been high for the few days we'd been apart. His skin was patchy and his hair was greasy, his right eye twitchy as it always was when he was on the chalk. When he opened his mouth to say hello, I could smell the speed eating away at his insides. Still, he was in a sweet mood. He picked me up and spun me around.

"Get in the truck!" Darryl said, breathing his decay on me.

His band mates studied me up and down. *Wuulves,* I thought to myself. *All of them.* We made a pit stop for genuine El Paso tacos and headed over to the guitarist's house. I threw my luggage in a back bedroom, then rejoined the gang in the living room, where a baggie of cocaine was being chopped into fine lines on an old coffee table.

"Come on, don't be shy, girl." Darryl shoved a rolled up dollar bill in my hand. I stared down at the drugs. It almost made me sick to look at them. After the Playboy debacle I had become animalistic. I'd tried to make myself feel better with the chemicals, but it had just been making things worse. I knew that I needed to slow down. I'd been clean since the day Darryl left. Well... one line wouldn't hurt. I snorted it off the table and felt the old familiar sting and drip in my throat. I snorted back another. Darryl snorted back two and threw me across his lap. I Eskimo-kissed him.

"My baby," he said, holding me tight.

At seven o' clock we all made our way to the venue. The boys played a blistering set and were well-received by a mob of eager fans happy to have their hometown boys back in action. After their set, we watched a bit of Judas Priest before heading back to the house to party some more with fans and groupies in tow. I thought Los Angeles had drugs, but El

Paso... El Paso had sacks of drugs and loads of eager customers. There wasn't much else to do in that dust bowl. Everyone laid their wares out on the table. We sniffed our powder and guzzled Southern Comfort and Coca Cola. Darryl stared at me from across the room, twitching, then marched over and grabbed me by my arm.

"Why were you looking at that guy at the club tonight?" he hissed in my ear, his breath as dry as the desert that surrounded us.

"What do you mean?"

"Don't play dumb with me, whore. You Playboy bunny whore. I saw it."

"Darryl, I didn't look at anybody." I searched my memory for anyone that I might've even glanced at, but there was no one. We were in Hell Paso for chrissake. I had been completely taken with my boyfriend that evening. Darryl had the onstage presence and voice of a metal god. He had amazed and inspired me. I'd tried to tell him after the show that if we could just get off the junk he could really be somebody. I knew I could, too.

He squeezed my arm so hard that I thought it would turn to mush in his big hands.

"Owwwww!"

"You embarrassed me in front of my friends!"

I looked around the room at the leaches and drug addicts that surrounded us.

"These people aren't your friends, Darryl, they're your fans. They'll tell you anything you want to hear, as long as there's plenty of drugs, booze, and whores around you."

He slapped me in the face, knocking me backwards just far enough to have a reason to yank me back up by my arm. He hustled me down the hallway, throwing me in the back bedroom where I'd stashed my suitcase earlier in the evening, and shut the door behind me. I tried to open it but he held his weight against it and I heard the sound of furniture being moved. He was barricading me in. I pounded on the door. Surely one of his idiot friends would let me out...

"The more you yell, the longer you'll be in there!" His voice was muffled by the wall of furniture he'd constructed but I could hear the party music had been turned off.

Darryl was making a joke of me. I heard laughter and then the music turned back on. I screamed and pounded on the door. No one came to my rescue.

I'd been stuck in there for three hours when I decided he probably wasn't going to let me out that night. I had to piss. My suitcase and cell phone were in the room with me but my purse was out front with my ATM card, one credit card and about twenty dollars in cash. Hell, it was probably gone by then anyway, judging by the amount of derelicts in the front room. Luckily, I had my license in my right pants pocket from the show. Okay, breathe. Who could I call? Not my parents. Not my Los Angeles friends, I'd never hear the end of it. I'd call Joey. Joey was an old boyfriend I'd left behind when I'd moved to Los Angeles from Detroit. His candle for me still burned.

He'd help.

Joey answered after two rings. "Autumn?"

"Hey. I need some help. I would never ask if---"

"Where are you?"

"El Paso. I just want to go home."

"Detroit home? Here?" Joey's voice on the other end was hopeful.

"No... Los Angeles. Can you buy me a plane ticket to Los Angeles? I swear I'll pay you back."

There was silence on the other end.

"It's that fucking guy you're dating, isn't it? He's going to kill you one day."

"I swear it, I swear I'll pay you back."

"Alright. But I'll call your mother if you don't stop this shit."

"Fine."

"Let me call the airline. I'll call you back in ten minutes."

It was the longest ten minutes of my life. When the phone finally rang I was so excited that it flew out of my hands before I could answer it.

"Hello?"

"You're fucking lucky."

"I'll kiss your ass next time I go home to Detroit, Joey."

"You're on a flight leaving at 6 a.m. to LAX. Fucking get there. "

"I owe you."

"More than you know. I love—"

I hung up the phone and cradled it in my hand for a minute.

There was one window in the room that was big enough for me and my suitcase to fit through. I tried to slide it open and nothing happened. The damn thing had been painted over. I tried again to no avail and fell to the ground in heaving sobs. The music in the other room was still loud. I took a deep breath, threw my suitcase through the glass of the window, then jumped out after it.

The El Paso air blew dank and dirty around me. I ran down the street towards the lights of an intersection. About a half mile down the road there was a 7-11 parking lot. A boy stood out front, smoking a cigarette. He could've been an axe murderer or a serial killer, but one thing he wasn't was Darryl Fucking Briggs.

"Hey. I lost my purse. I don't have any money. I really need a ride to the airport."

The stranger eye-fucked me, flicked his cigarette to the ground, and opened up his passenger door. I jumped in. Three hours later, I was on a plane home with a number I'd never call in my pocket.

22.

THE DEEP SLEEP

STRIPPED OF MY PLAYBOY TV CONTRACT after one hundred episodes, I was back to being a full-time peeler. I started working at a strip club in Downtown Los Angeles. I also often found myself curled up next to Richard under the sheets in a Super Eight motel off the 110 Freeway. His belly rose and fell softly against my back. The TV buzzed in front of us. I was happy that he'd left it on. Usually he kept it off so that it wouldn't distract me from paying attention to him. I fingered the bedspread. Outside, work trucks could be heard pulling up, parking, and pulling out again.

"My son doesn't want to go to UC Santa Barbara anymore, he wants to come home," Richard said.

"Of course he wants to come home, it's his first semester. It's a new thing for him," I said.

"He's going to come back home and go to Cal State instead."

"That's stupid. He'd rather have a degree from a state school than a university? If it was my kid, I'd make him stay the full year," I said flipping over to look at Richard.

His lower lip jutted out. He'd recently had a giant mole lasered off of his face. I missed it. It gave me something to focus on while I danced for him.

"Well, he's not going to." Richard sat up and took a noisy pull off of his water bottle before crushing it in his big hands.

"He's fucking spoiled. You spoil him." I got off the bed and started to put my clothes back on. "I have to be up really early for an audition tomorrow, " I said, lying. "Commercial thing."

"Okay, but if you leave early you're not getting a tip."

I shrugged my shoulders. I wanted to be anywhere but there with him in that room, listening to his rich, libertarian, male problems.

"Can you believe I've known you over half a decade? And you just get prettier!"

I winced at the way the words formed on his lips. It had been six years since I found his car keys at the Century Lounge. Almost 10 since I'd started dancing back in Detroit.

"I love you," he said, cupping my face in his hands.

I smiled at him and shook my face out of his hands. "All right. I got to go now. I'll see you next week?"

"Absolutely." He counted off four hundred-dollar bills for me and I hugged him goodbye. He stood on the balcony of the hotel and watched as I drove away.

The 110 Freeway home was a straight shot in my

Harley Davidson Truck. I loved that truck bought with a five-thousand-dollar down payment funded by Richard and Playboy TV. It was chilly but I liked the windows down. The hotel room had been as airless as Richard's stale wit, as fluorescent as the white of his thighs. I wanted to take the California night air down deep into my lungs. Despite the recent turn of events, I knew she still had something in store for me. She had to.

That's the thing about California: If you just hold on long enough, you can conquer her.

Darryl's car was still in the driveway when I got home. I fixed my lip-gloss in my rear view mirror before getting out. I'd been thinking about him the whole time I was with Richard, hoping that he'd still be waiting for me at my house. I'd given him a set of keys. I'd forgiven him for the whole El Paso incident. He would've let me out of that room, I knew he would have, eventually. Maybe it had even been my own fault. We still fought all the time, but at least he made me feel... *something.*

Most of the time I felt absolutely nothing. I'd tried to feel, I really had. I'd fucked all sorts of supposedly wonderful men: The tall and handsome son of the Peruvian Minister of Defense who showed me Machu Picchu. The A & R guy that took me to all of my favorite rock 'n' roll shows. The writer of the Playboy TV show I'd worked on. The music producer, the drummer, the trainer...

They were all lovely guys, and I tried, I did, but they latched on like dryer sheets clinging to my pants legs, latched on and tried to change the things they'd initially swooned over. Dancing was who I was, I told myself; it was how I supported myself. I'd been taking care of myself for a decade, and I wasn't stopping for anyone. It was easier to exterminate them and find someone else to fuck.

The only real loyalty I'd assumed in all that time, through all the men, was to my Blue Heeler, Bianca. I saved her from extermination at the North Valley Shelter and she loved me desperately.

I opened the door to my apartment. Darryl sat on my couch, blankly staring at Pamela Anderson gabbing at David Letterman on *The Late Night Show*. His stringy hair had pasted itself to his forehead. Bianca cut her eyes at him from her dog bed on the floor. They had a general disdain for each other. He didn't say hello, didn't look over to me. I sat next to him on the couch.

"Where did you put the rest of the coke?" he asked.

"We ran out, remember?"

He clicked off the television and sat there silently, sweat rolling down his brow. He smelled chemical. I knew he'd been doing speed all day.

"Where the fuck is rest of the coke?" he asked, still staring straight ahead.

"I swear, Darryl, I don't have—"

He jumped up, grabbed me by the throat and squeezed. Bianca barked and snapped at his ankles, howling as he kicked her out of his way.

"You give me all the drugs you have or I'm going

to call the cops and tell them that you have drugs hidden in here and they'll come take your ass to jail, you goddamn Playboy half-breed bunny." He switched his grip from my neck to my right arm, pulling me across the hardwood floor to my bedroom. He'd already emptied out all of my dresser drawers on to the floor.

"Stop, just stop," I sobbed. "I'll give it to you!" I went to my closet. In the corner, there was a tiny piece of carpet that folded back. I felt around for a twenty-dollar bag of cocaine from underneath it and threw it at him. "THERE! JUST FUCKING GO!"

Darryl fingered the drugs in his hands. I sat in the corner of the room, staring back at him. He walked towards me. He would apologize, I knew it. He'd be sorry. He'd do a line and calm down. He extended a hand to me and helped me up. He took a long look at me, then sucker punched the right side of my face. I fell back against the wall.

"Don't ever fucking lie to me." He pocketed the drugs and took off in his Pathfinder.

I was too tired to cry about the imminent black eye as I stared at myself in the mirror. I took a long, hot shower and got into my bed, but sleep was eluding me. I knew it was wrong, but I missed him. He was the only person I had. I shouldn't have hid the drugs from him.

I got out of bed, went back to my hiding spot, and fished out my last dime bag of cocaine. I laid out four lines on my nightstand, about half a baggie. I stared at it and then looked back in the mirror at myself.

A purple bruise had begun to bulge around my eye. *I fucking deserve this*, I thought to myself. *I deserve every scar he put on me.* I was a junky piece of shit. I wanted out of this life. I didn't have anything or anyone. I'd fucked up everything good in my life, and it was my own goddamn fault.

I thought about how the barrel of a gun might taste in my mouth: metallic and cold like cheap fucking silverware. I laughed that my final thought before blowing my head off would be about Sizzler silverware. Then I made a split-second decision. I snorted back the four lines I'd laid out, then took the rest of the baggie of drugs and flushed it down the toilet. I was fucking done with that part of my life. Things were going to be different.

I started to reassemble the drawers that Darryl had ransacked. I organized my closet and cleaned the bathroom and vacuumed. By the time I was done it was near one a.m. and my buzz had dwindled. I started to regret throwing my drugs away. I checked the toilet just in case the baggie had floated back up. No such luck.

I lit a candle, got in bed, and tried to sleep again. I lay awake for an hour before getting out of bed and digging around by my nightstand for any leftover crumbs of cocaine that Darryl had missed. I found two small nuggets, covered in dog fur and carpet debris, and chopped them up into a little line that I snorted back. A wave of relief fell over me. But I knew that the high would only last a few minutes. I was restless. Maybe...

Maybe I could do just one more twenty bag that night and then never again. That would be it.

I called my dealer up.

"Hello?" Jonny's New York accent cut through the phone line.

"Hey, it's Autumn. I just wondered if you were up and if I could come by?"

"Only for you... call me when you're out front. Make it fast."

I knew I shouldn't have made the call. Now I'd HAVE to go. And Jonny would try to put his dick in me. Bianca lay next to me in the bed. She put her paw on my chest, her way of telling me to go back to sleep. I pushed her off, threw on my sweat pants, and got in my truck. It was a five-minute drive to his house. I put on Velvet Revolver and sped down Burbank Boulevard. I sang along with Scott Weiland, looking in to my rear view mirror at my purple eye. It wasn't so bad. It would be okay; I would be okay.

When I looked back at the road there was a minivan stopped dead in front of me. There was nowhere to go; no time to slow down. The violent crunch of metal meeting metal at 60 MPH filled my ears. My truck's front end crumpled, thrusting the minivan down the street. The windshield imploded, showering me with glass as my face pressed into the air bag.

Now this, this was something! This felt real.

Fuck everything else. Fuck everyone. Fuck my father, fuck Danny Hunt, fuck Darryl, and fuck all the latte-drinking whores that called themselves my friends while we shoveled drugs up our noses. Fuck every piece of shit that thought the crumpled twenty-dollar bill in their hand let them own me. Fuck Hollywood, the big machine that brought me here just to grind me up and spit me out.

There was blood. Shards of glass and white powder floated around me. It was the most beautiful thing I had ever seen. Then there was nothing. Silence. Now I could sleep. Goddamn, it had been a long time since I slept.

23.

MEMENTO MORI
Cypress College Mortuary Department
One year later

"FUCK. I KNEW IT. ANOTHER FUCKING nigger!" Tracy pulled aside her mouth cover with a blue surgical-gloved hand and spit into the sink. "Why do they always have to be niggers?"

She peeled back the rest of the body bag, revealing the remains of an emaciated brown body. I touched the mold on the old man's face in front of us. A thick cloud rested over his pupils, reminding me of the sunny side down eggs I'd had for breakfast. The tag wrapped around his toe read "Roderick Jones."

We were six months into mortuary college. Embalming labs were every Wednesday and Friday in the unfortunate time slot that came just before lunch. At 10 a.m., we would dab Vick's Vapo Rub underneath our noses and change into our Personal Protective Equipment: Chemical resistant coveralls, surgical masks, industrial strength gloves, and booties that fit over our shoes. Then we would shuffle into the lab and begin the dubious task of removing unclaimed bodies from the Los Angeles County morgue from their body bags.

Underneath the heavy plastic, the smell of putrefaction was thick. Some of the corpses were so rotten that they were impossible to practice our budding embalming skills on. The especially foul bodies were wrapped back up immediately as we tried our best to recover from the pungent smell, disfigured faces, and liquefied flesh we had witnessed. Mold, skin slip, and bedsores that ate cavities clear through backs were lesser evils that we could handle. After we had poked, prodded, bathed, and embalmed our corpses, they were sent back to their spot in the county morgue, where they'd rot a little slower than their un-embalmed, indigent freezer buddies.

Tracy was a stripper like me, but she was from Las Vegas. Her hair hung in oily black ropes past her shoulders and her skin was shiny and pitted. We first met in our Monday morning Thanatology class, where she sat two rows in front and three rows over from me. Tracy spent most of class picking at her pimples in a tiny cubic-zirconia encrusted mirror. Her brown eyes turned to reptile slits when I passed her by in class, until the day that I paid her a compliment on a pink sweater she was wearing. I knew how to soften up girls like Tracy. Fate, or a professor that liked to see two girls bent over a corpse together, had made us lab partners.

I stood over ol' Roderick and set to work at scraping his beard of green mold off. I clipped his finger and toenails and cleaned out his ears and nose with swabs of cotton on long hooked dressing forceps. His nose crunched as I went deep. A steady stream of shit dripped from his ass. When I was sure he was near empty, I used an A/V plug to close him off. Now that he was clean, it was time to embalm him.

It had been a year since my accident, a year since I touched drugs, a year since I discovered that the Cypress Mortuary college existed. I had been in love with death my whole life, so it seemed a natural decision to enroll.

I had to adjust quickly to the demands of the Embalming program. Classes began at 8 a.m. sharp, no absences allowed. I hadn't been up at 8 a.m. save for an audition or two in a decade, much less 6 a.m., to accommodate for the hour-plus drive to campus. Chemistry, Mortuary Law, Accounting, Anatomy, Physiology, and Embalming courses left no time for coke binges; no time to feel ill after being up all night. In that way, the corpses I surrounded myself with had been saving my life. Keeping my nose clean.

Linear and anatomical guides became my new obsession. When I wanted the blow, I would get out my flashcards. Sometimes, I'd turn it into a little song that I'd sing over and over again in my head.

"The femoral artery passes through the center of the femoral triangle and is bounded laterally by the medial border of the Sartorius muscle and medially by the abductor longus muscle. "

"Nice incision." My professor nodded with approval at my precision with a scalpel as I sliced into

Roderick's thigh.

I winked at my corpse as I separated fascia from muscle tissue. "Roderick, you look amazing," I whispered, squeezing his hand. "Handsome as fuck, I swear it." I inserted an embalming tube in his femoral artery, and a drain tube in the accompanying vein. While the fluid filled him, I stroked his arm, and made sure his eye caps were secure. I rubbed massage cream on his leathery face.

"If there's another nigger, I'm not doing it. I won't touch it." Tracy's eyes darted at me.

I smiled at her. Her words didn't bother me. Tracy's own father was dying. He was rotting away from cancer, and she was rotting away from crystal meth. And the corpse in front of us, old Roderick Jones with his gangrenous leg and bed sores, was already dead. *Memento Mori.* We were all going to die, baby.

24.

CINNAMON ROLLS

MY DAYS WERE COMPLETELY CONSUMED with stiffs. I had stiff corpses during the day at Cypress College and stiff dicks to writhe on at night at Sam's Hof Brau. When the club was slow, I would sit with my legs folded under me in a lap dance booth studying my embalming textbooks. When I did have a client, I entertained myself while I entertained them by deciding what their fate would be. Perhaps they'd be following a work truck too closely on the freeway in their convertible, back end filled to the brim with unintentional instruments of death. A chain would come unlatched, sending debris straight through their cranium. As I danced, my customers bled and became disfigured.

Once in awhile during a lap dance the conversation would be passable and I'd forget to kill them off for a few moments. Then they'd mention their wife or their perfect girlfriend. I wanted to ask them why, then—why were they there? Why did they just give me 100 dollars to grind on their cock and giggle in their ear for five songs if their spouse was so incredible? I had given up on men completely.

Then I came across another kind of Stiff altogether.

I was dancing on top of a table at Sam's Hof Brau, dodging plates of hot wings with my acrylic heels when I locked eyes with a brown-eyed boy named Dylan Stiff. He sat with a group of friends two tables down, and when he looked up at me, I felt safe for the brief instant that I was captured in his vision. It was the first time in a long time that I had felt that way. I walked around the club at least three times before I had the guts to say "hello."

"Hi," I stuck out my hand awkwardly.

He gazed up at me and gave me a cocky smile. "I've seen you here before," he said. He was more soft spoken than his lips had led me to believe.

"Really? I've never seen you."

"We call you the Glamazon because of all that hair. And you're so tan. "

"Glamazon? That makes me feel six feet tall. I'm only five foot two." I looked down at the gum-spackled Hof Brau floor. "So... if you've seen me here before, how come you never said 'hi'?"

"I don't know. You're always busy. Like tonight, you were on top of that fat guy's table for an hour." He patted the seat next to him. "Do you have 10 minutes for me? I'm Dylan."

Fuck. Rent was due. I needed to make my rounds and make my cash. But somehow I didn't care. I sat down. I left the club that night without my rent money, but the beautiful boy had my number.

Dylan rolled up in a candy apple red 1969 Cadillac to pick me up on our first date. He had had my number for a week before he dialed it. I wasn't a fan of people that made the first phone call into a game, and I almost told him I wasn't interested. But when I heard the old engine pull up outside and caught a glimpse of it out my window, I was glad that I had said "yes." I giggled as I watched him walk around his car a few times to make sure that it was perfect. The boy had swagger. I grabbed my purse and went outside to meet him.

"Nice ride for a country boy," I said, smiling at him.

"I saw you peeking out the window at it," he said.

I blushed. Had I looked too long? He opened up the passenger door for me and I slid onto the slick red leather seats. We drove around the neighborhood like royalty, stopping for lunch at an outdoor café, and everyone stared as we made our way out of the big red beast.

"So tell me about your school," I said, as Dylan pulled out my chair.

"I go to the Art Center in Pasadena. I'm studying industrial design."

"I know the Art Center! It's one of the best schools in the country!" I was impressed. Only the best of the best went to the Art Center.

"Two Arnold Palmers," Dylan signaled to a waitress. "How do you know the Art Center?"

"Well, once upon a time I went to art school, too.

CCS in Detroit. I even got a big fat scholarship. But, I mean, that was a long time ago. I wanted to move to Hollywood and—"

"Wait, you went to CCS? My god! That's a great school! So, how come you're a stripper?"

I could feel the blood run to my face. The age-old question.

"Well, I wanted to do other things. I'm in school now. I go to embalming school." I suddenly felt worthless.

Dylan smiled his cocky smile from across the table at me.

"An embalmer, eh? So if we got married," he said, "you'd be a mortician named Autumn Stiff." He laughed.

"I guess I would be! I like it," I giggled, and looked away from his gaze. I knew that if I stared back too long, sooner or later his brains would be on the wall behind him.

We pulled back up in front of my house just before sunset.

"Do you want to come in?" I asked him. I was still first-date giddy.

"Sure," he nodded.

I opened the front door and sat on the couch with the beautiful boy beside me. I reached out for his hand and felt his fingers in mine. They were shredded and rough from working on his Cadillac. A desire came over me to wrap myself around him, and I hopped onto his lap, curling up on him like an alley cat that had been out all night. Bianca instinctively followed suit, and we were like two warm cinnamon rolls holding the poor boy down. We were not worried that it would dissuade him from coming back. We knew he was ours. I felt a wave of calm fall over me. I could sense that his world was still and I'd be able to walk about in it without fear of being trampled.

25.

BENDING FROM THE WAIST

DYLAN AND I HAD BEEN TOGETHER FOR two months when we booked a trip to Bellingham, Washington, so that I could meet his parents. Until we pulled up to the long, curved driveway of Dylan's father's house, I'd been blissfully sweeping our differences under the rug. When his father, stepmother, and two golden-haired sisters—one with a perfect husband and adorable children—stepped out to greet us with a Retriever in tow, I was suddenly aware of exactly how different we were.

"This is Autumn." Dylan pushed me towards his father. The senior Stiff shook my hand up and down awkwardly, eyeing me with curiosity. His hands were clammy and he wiped them on his Khaki slacks after our encounter.

The afternoon was spent making small talk with the golden crew while Dylan and his father worked on an old Morgan in the shed together. That evening, we all drove to Dylan's grandmother's for supper with the rest of the family. Because "supper" was what you had in such places, never "dinner."

Dylan's aunt, who had given him the red Caddy he had picked me up in on our first date, eyed me from across the room, glass of wine in a teetering hand. A portrait of her and her horse, commissioned when she was sixteen, hung on the wall above her head. Next to her portrait was a portrait of Dylan's father by the same artist.

Crab legs were served for supper, and the fine china and silverware were laid out. Crab legs were a dubious task on their own, and not one I'd enjoy taking on in front of people I had never met before.

I tried to make light of my dire situation. "You are brave leaving a girl who can barely use a knife and a fork to eat crab legs," I said, and laughed.

Everyone stared at me. Dylan's younger sister giggled. I wasn't sure if it was in jest or to lighten the cloud that had settled around me.

We ate our crab legs in the strange silence that white families often eat in. Every knock of a crystal glass, every clink of a fork threatened to expose my secret: I shouldn't fucking be there. I just didn't belong.

After dinner, I offered to clear the plates. Dylan's aunt, who had sipped her wine through dinner as if she was sipping the blood of Christ, accompanied me.

"I want you to know, Autumn," she started, "that I'm so glad that you are here."

"Well, thank you," I said, scraping food off plates into the trash.

She staggered towards me and put her hand

on my shoulder for balance. "And... I just want you to know... that I can teach you how to properly use a knife and fork; I'll do that for you. You know, my parents sent me to etiquette school, and I will gladly share my knowledge. "

I blushed a hot red. She thought that I had been serious? "Thank you... so much." She released my shoulder, smiling coyly, just like the girl in the portrait on her mommy and daddy's wall.

When I went back to the living room to join the rest of the family, they stared back at me, an unblinking wall of judgment.

"Let's hit the road," Dylan said. He already had his leather jacket on and mine draped over his arm. He thrust it at me. "Ready?"

I said my goodbyes to his family, smiling, and we hopped in our rental. Dylan was quiet. I grabbed for his hand.

"We're going back to Seattle tonight," he said. "I just want to get out of here and go have some fun in the city."

"Is everything alright?"

"It's perfect, Autumn. Everything is fucking perfect."

We drove to Seattle and set up camp in an apartment that reeked of cat piss that his stepdad kept in the city when he wanted to avoid long drives home to Bellingham... or when he wanted to fuck one of his coworkers. But that was another story altogether. Dylan was quiet. The smell of cat piss permeated the air, punctuated our conversation.

"My dad wants me to break up with you. He says that if I don't, he won't pay for my school anymore. They saw your website."

That. I stiffened in the bed beside him. I had recently started a pay site to cash in on some of the fame from my Playboy days. I didn't think it was a big deal. For $19.99 a month a man could take a gander at some nudie pictures of me. Was this 25-year-old really going to leave me because his father didn't approve?

"Autumn, my school is 45,000 dollars a year. I'm crazy about you but I don't know what to do."

I searched my head for something else I could have done to make his family disapprove. I had dressed smartly. I had been courteous. I had been overly thankful as I said my goodbyes to them. I'd hugged his father and his stepmother. I seethed at the thought of how they must have cringed when I touched them, pictures of my shaved vagina flashing back in their heads. I pictured his prim stepmother washing her hands furiously after we left. We lay next to each other, not touching, quiet in the blue black of the apartment.

"I'll take down my website," I finally said. "I'll just take it down." The words flew out of my mouth, and they were a surprise to even me.

"What about dancing?"

"I can't..."

He was quiet at first. And then, "Well, the website for sure. You're too good for that shit, anyways. You don't need to do that."

He leaned on his elbow and looked over at me. I snuggled up to him and he scratched my head between the tracks of my extensions. I battle-readied my heart. I felt a competition coming on and I wasn't going to lose. I wasn't going to lose this boy that cooked for me, held my hand. Deep inside, however, I knew our relationship had forever changed.

The next day at the Seattle airport, I dropped my water bottle and bent over to pick it up. Dylan grabbed at my wrist.

"Jesus, Autumn, bend from your knees, not your waist," he hissed in my ear. "You look like a fucking stripper. It's embarrassing!"

26.

GET A REAL JOB

IN THE SUMMER OF 2007, I PUT ON A BLUE cap and gown and collected my degree in Mortuary Science as my parents and Dylan looked on. I graduated on the Dean's list and passed my National and State board exams with flying colors. When my license came in the mail, I felt its paper in my hand and read the words stretched across the page, but still had a hard time believing them to be true. I'd finished something that I had started, and I had done it well. I was a licensed mortician.

"You can get a real job now," Dylan reminded on a daily basis, usually over breakfast.

I put the cereal box between us, stared down into my bowl of Honey Smacks, and sighed. My certificates and degree were tucked away in a blue leather binder in our nightstand. They were pretty to look at, but who was I kidding? Who would give me a job? I had no experience. I had Playboy TV, Sam's Hof Brau, and a nudie website on my resume, for chrissake. I didn't know how to get a job without auditioning in a pair of acrylic heels for it.

After Dylan left for work, I searched my computer for the resume I'd made in my business class at Cypress College. My name looked official in the boldface font I had chosen. I printed it up on eggshell linen paper and wrote a cover letter stressing my passion for the industry. That afternoon, I dropped off my resume to 10 local mortuaries.

Two days later, I got a call back from a Catholic mortuary in Ladera Heights. I had an interview!

Early on a Monday, I donned a Theory business suit that had cost me one night's earnings from stripping at Sam's Hof Brau to interview for a position that would pay me what my suit cost in two long weeks, and drove down to Ladera Heights. Holy Cross was a sprawling cemetery with a funeral home smack dab in the middle. Bela Lugosi and Sharon Tate were buried here, as well as Bing Crosby and Darby Crash. Even John Candy had a spot in the wall of their mausoleum.

My interviewer had a bulbous nose and white hair that curled around his ears. He smiled when he rounded the corner and saw me waiting for him.

"Oh!" he said, rubbing his hand on his cheap suit.

"I'm Autumn." I extended a hand as he reddened. He smiled so hard that his pockmarks squeezed together.

He took me to his office, sat me in a leather chair facing his, and put on a pair of black-rimmed glasses. He held my resume in both hands and scanned it intently. I started to sweat. This whole thing was stupid. Who was I kidding? He finally looked up at me.

"Dean's list! That's great," he said. "You must be a smart cookie."

"Just a hard worker," I said. And that definitely wasn't a lie.

"The position we have available is running the viewings at night... does that sound like something you'd be interested in?"

"Definitely!"

"How about if you come in on Wednesday for paperwork, and we'll get you started right away."

"I'd love to!" His hand shook mine vigorously up and down. I had a job.

Back in my car, I called Dylan's cell phone.

"Hello," he answered in hushed tones. I knew he was busy working.

"Hey." I tried to sound as dejected as possible.

"How did it go?"

"Eh... I don't know."

"Well, you shouldn't have worn that suit! It was a bit much, don't you..."

"I got the job, Dylan."

"You got it?"

"Yes!" I squealed, despite the doubt in his voice buzzing in my ears.

27.

HISPANIC PANIC

"WAIT UNTIL YOU SEE THE HISPANIC panic," Melissa said, raising a penciled-in eyebrow.

"It'll get you every time." Sean crossed his arms and puffed out his bird chest. "You have to be tough. I mean really tough! Just close the casket, walk away."

I liked my new coworkers immediately. A Goth girl with lanky hair and glasses, and an aspiring fire-boy were to show me the ropes my first night at Holy Cross Mortuary and Cemetery. That evening we had two viewings: A Filipino family and a stone-faced Caucasian family.

The lounge area overflowed with the pungent smells of a Filipino feast of mourning. The white women making their way to viewing room number four covered their tiny plastic noses in horror.

The viewings at Holy Cross fascinated me as much as my grandfather's had many years before. The chemical-filled dead looked sharp in their fancy suits and dresses that they hadn't had a use for while they were alive. Their faces were painted so heavily that their own grandchildren couldn't recognize them. Their families moaned and wailed and then nodded in agreement that, yes, the embalmer had done a great job. And the Catholics... they would do it for days before they could bring themselves to actually put the damn corpse in the ground. For a bunch of people that believed so fully in a magical sky world where life would be better tenfold, they sure had a hard time letting go.

This death thing had become as broken as marriage had. There was a time when it was welcome at home; the sick were comforted and surrounded by their families as they passed. They died in the same bed that they had made their children in. Somewhere along the way, death had become a crippling fear, the end of the American dream. The healthcare industry had made it an ugly thing that hooked Grandma and Grandpa up to a big machine. And who wanted to look at that? Better to let them go and not think about it too much, better to sweep it under the rug, shut it away behind a nursing room door.

I'd been at the mortuary for a week when my manager gave me a set of heavy gold keys and left me alone to handle a charity viewing for an old Mexican. His church had paid for his services and burial, kindly placing him in the cheapest casket they could purchase; a compressed cardboard number that was almost passable from 10 feet away. He was brown and wrinkled in his baby blue box, surrounded by his family.

"Close the casket exactly at eight p.m.," my boss said as we watched the family from the doorway of the chapel. "Even if people are still gathered around it. If you don't, they'll never leave."

My blood ran cold. Maybe I wasn't ready. I turned to object to my solitude that evening, but my boss was already gone.

At 7:55 p.m. I gingerly made my way towards the casket. It was still surrounded by throngs of sobbing family members. I forced my way to the front of the blue cardboard box, elbowing people like I was at a sold-out rock concert. Positioning myself in front of it, I cleared my throat. "Thank you for coming to the Rodriguez viewing tonight," I said as assertively as I could muster. "We will be closing the doors in five minutes so please pay your final respects and exit the building. Services will be held at 9 a.m. tomorrow morning."

No one moved. No one pretended they were going to. Brown arms shoved past me and into the casket.

"The viewing is over for the evening," I repeated, and changed my stance to that of a raging mother lion. The sobs grew louder. Women clutched at the dead man in the casket. So this was what my co-workers had warned me of. I had a full-blown case of the Hispanic panic on my hands. I would have to be relentless.

I dodged the arms and reached for the top of the casket to pull it down, but it stuck. I pulled harder. Nothing. I gave one last strong pull, and the lid of the casket groaned as its hinges weakened, released, and snapped. My cheeks burned. Poor old Mexican... He had worked hard his whole life, just to have a girl in a suit that cost more than his entire funeral break his casket.

I scrabbled to pick the lid up off of the floor, and propped it on top like ill-fitting Tupperware, before regaining my authoritative role in front of it. To my surprise, the crowd began to retreat. They trickled out the doors solemnly until it was just me, the dead Mexican, and my carpet sweeper.

I kicked off my pumps, collected the snotty tissues and Doritos bags left under the seats in the chapel, and vacuumed the carpet. After I was done, I moved Mr. Rodriguez to the back room where he would wait to be wheeled out for his 9 a.m. service the following morning. I lifted the top of his casket, looked down at him, and stroked his forehead and hands. The dead were so peaceful.

"I'm so sorry about your casket," I said. "I'm new. I'm still learning. And don't worry, your family will be back tomorrow." I replaced the lid properly, hoping my boss wouldn't notice my mishap the next morning.

There was only one other body in the back room that evening. I opened a casket and peered in on a little, over-embalmed infant with a glob of pink lipstick on her rosebud mouth. There was no one else around... what could it hurt? I lifted her out and cradled her in my arms. I didn't want the bodies to feel lonely after their families had left them for the evening under my care. Loneliness was one thing I definitely understood.

28.

THE DEATH SURROUND

"THERE'S SOMETHING IN MY DAD'S CAS-
ket that smells really bad." A teenaged girl
stood in front of me, arms crossed, chewing her gum.
I had just arrived at Holy Cross for my shift. Apparently it was doomed to be a trying day.

"Let me go see what's going on," I said with a
smile, dreading the possibilities that awaited me.
Overflow bodies were embalmed at a sister mortuary
and brought over every morning. If they had screwed
something up so that this body was rotting and foul
for the viewing and funeral, we could have a nice little lawsuit on our hands.

The girl's sister and mother were waiting for us
in viewing room three. They were stoic as they stood
in front of their husband and father's casket. It wasn't
a new thing for them; their father was absent often on
fishing trips. On this last one, he had met his fate, and
was found waterlogged and belly-up on his boat. Due
to the circumstances, he had spent some time at the
coroner's office. By the time he lay in his Sunday suit

in the metal box in front of me, he'd been dead at least a month.

Drowning victims were usually pretty nasty, but this fellow looked dapper, not a trace of purple in his face. It had been effectively removed by a skilled embalmer. So where was the pungent smell—more chemical than rot—coming from? I opened the lower half of the casket and had my answer: A plastic bag of the fisherman's organs was nestled at his feet. I tried to close the casket before the family saw the bag but it was too late.

"What's that?" The youngest daughter grabbed at the fragrant bag, lifting it into the air. Usually autopsied bodies were embalmed from the inside out, and afterwards, the organs were placed back in the body. Had the embalmer been careless? Had he not had enough room to put the waterlogged organs back? Whatever excuse I could muster wouldn't be good enough for a grieving family. I'd have to be honest.

"Usually they put the organs back inside after an autopsy," I explained carefully. "I'm not sure why the embalmer couldn't but I'm sure he had a good reason. I'm going to put these away in our back room until after the ceremony and rest assured he will be buried with them. Is there anything else I can do for you before your viewing starts?" Gently, I took the bag away from the young girl in front of me. There was silence for a moment.

"Can I feel the weight of that bag?" the mother asked. "I mean, out of curiosity..."

"Well, sure..." I handed her the bag, nervous that my boss would walk in on me juggling the organs with the clients.

"Me too," said the other daughter.

After they'd each had a turn with Daddy's organs, they handed them back to me, and in my Theory suit, I carried a bag of viscera down the hallway and to the refrigerator.

Every day at Holy Cross was an adventure. Often, I'd have poorly embalmed ship-ins from Mexico City purging from the mouth to fix. One day, I had to organize the viewings for both parties in a case where a man had stabbed his wife to death and then killed himself. Another afternoon, I helped a single father decorate the chapel for his 14-year-old daughter's viewing.

Some days were harder than others.

"Melissa just called in sick today, kid, you're on your own tonight!" my boss called after me one evening as I arrived for my shift, late as usual.

"Okay! No problem; got it covered!"

I opened my folder with the days viewing assignments laid out for me and froze. *Today of all days, Melissa? Really?* She was leaving me alone for the mother load of viewings. A fucking toddler! I'd be all alone for the viewing of a three-year-old Hispanic boy whose father had rolled their car in the middle of the night on a drive from Sacramento to Los Angeles. His wife had been in the passenger seat and was eight months pregnant. They lost *both* their unborn child and their toddler in the accident. The wife wouldn't be at the funeral for her little boy. She hadn't yet woken from her coma. When she finally did wake up, she'd realize that both of her sons were dead.

I wanted to throw up.

I went to the backroom and opened the little boy's casket before wheeling him out to the viewing room. His skin was soft and olive, and his eyelashes fell against his check, long and black. There were no signs of trauma, no bruises. He was a beautiful sleeping angel. I fluffed his pillow, kissed him on the forehead and brought him to the front of the largest viewing room that we had.

At 6 p.m. the family started to pour into the lobby, bringing with them a wave of Hispanic panic. Grandmothers, grandfathers, uncles and aunties, cousins, neighborhood friends, and members of the community came to lament the loss of innocence. The boy's father was heavily sedated, and rocked back and forth in a chair in the front.

"My baby, my baby!" he wailed.

I was certain he could still see the blood on his own hands. Throughout the commotion, one boy went unnoticed. He sat in a corner by himself, sobbing. No one came to him. Relatives shuffled by him, absorbed in putting on a show of their own grief. When it was closing time, the boy still sat in the corner by himself.

"Is that your brother?" I asked, kneeling down beside him.

"No, my cousin." The boy rubbed his eyes with his fists and jutted out a tiny chin. Even in grief, his little boy Mexican machismo wanted to shine through for the strange lady in front of him. It failed. Tears dripped down his nose. "He was my best friend."

"That must be really hard to lose your best friend." I grabbed his hand in mine. "I have to close these doors now... but you know what? I bet you were very special to your cousin, too. I didn't see you talk to him all night. I bet he would really like it if you talked to him for a few minutes by yourself with no one else around. Would you like that?"

He nodded.

"Hold on. " I smiled at him. "I'll be right back."

I brought a step stool from the back room and placed it in front of the casket. "Go ahead, I'll leave you alone. But I'll be right outside the door if you need me."

The boy stepped on the stool, looking back at me. I nodded at him, then closed the door and watched through the glass as two best friends said goodbye to each other. I envied their connection. I wanted a best friend. Someone to hold my hand when I died, someone to give a fuck.

29.

ALEX

FROM THE DUSTY VELVET CURTAINS BE-hind the lap dance booths at the strip club, to the body bags and satin-lined caskets at Holy Cross, decay had begun to hang heavy in my nostrils. I thought that maybe, just maybe, it was time to give life a try. And by life, I meant the brief moments before death.

I found an ad for a hospice group looking for volunteers. I'd heard one of my professors talk about hospice; groups that offered palliative care for the terminally ill. It seemed like a shit job, watching someone rot in front of you, but the chance to get some sort of insight on my biggest fear was tempting. I called the number, and after a month of training, I was given a nametag and a briefcase that contained a supply kit of plastic gloves, hand sanitizer, and medical sheets.

My first assignment was a 90-year-old woman in a nursing home that was actively dying. Meaning she didn't have six months, or even three. She'd be gone within the week. The woman didn't have any family, so my supervisor asked if I would sit in vigil with her as she passed. It took me two days after getting the assignment to go through with it. I drove past the nursing home twice, too nervous to make the trip inside. What was I doing? What help could I be?

On the third day, I walked into the home, signed my name on a clipboard, and slowly made my way to room 130, not knowing if my patient would even still be there. I took a deep breath before walking in the door. There she was; white hair pulled away from her face in a neat bun, hospital bed enveloping her tiny body. Her skin was stretched a pearly transparent color over her closed eyes, and her body rose and fell in the tiniest breaths I'd ever seen. I unfolded a chair that leaned against the wall and pulled it up next to her. She opened her eyes and looked over at me. I held my breath. There was no alarm on her face, she seemed happy to see someone there. I reached for her hand.

"Hello... my name is Autumn. I'm here from your hospice. I'm here for anything you need." I stroked her hand as she studied my face. I was trying hard not to lose it.

A handwritten note taped on the wall next to her bed read, *"She likes makeup."* Underneath the note was a tube of red lipstick. I took the lipstick and put it on her lips as best as I could. The dying woman in front of me murmured in satisfaction... or maybe I imagined it. Her hand searched for mine on the sheet, and when we touched again, she closed her eyes, a faint smile on her freshly crimsoned mouth.

I closed my own eyes, and when I opened them,

she had passed away. I stared at her for a long while before I went to get anyone. I studied her hand, bruised by time, next to mine. How was it that she had ended up here alone, with a girl she didn't know holding her hand as she passed? What kind of life had she lived? Who had loved her? Who had hated her? Would I, too, die alone?

My next hospice case was very different. I was assigned to an elderly man with three months to live. I walked through the halls of the Glen Oaks nursing home looking for his room. Mortuary college and Holy Cross had taught me the smell of decomposition all too well, and death crept down the hallway beside me, in and out of the small rectangular windows on each door. Behind the doors, patients laid silent as corpses, open mouths sucking in the dank air in noisy rattles as they awaited a scythe-wielding reaper. *Two days left for this one,* I estimated, looking through the glass at a man. Less than 24 hours for another.

Holding my breath, I made it to room 120, knocked on the door, and let myself in. A wrinkled Armenian with a swollen nose sat with his spindly legs hanging off of his hospital bed, a wheeled tray of diced vegetables and chicken pushed in front of him. A glass of milk quivered on his tray. His hospital robe hung loosely around his sagging flesh. He peered at me with curiosity as he shoveled a spoon full of carrots and peas into his mouth. Half of them missed and settled into the folds of his baby blue hospital gown.

"Hi! I'm Autumn," I said, smiling. "I'm here from

your hospice to..." I didn't know what to say I was even doing there. I felt so crass. *Hi! I'm here to read to you while you rot away before you die!* Or, *Hey there, you've got less than six months to live so I'm here to make you think someone still cares once or twice a week.*

He watched me silently.

"I'm here to just come by and say hello," I finally finished, flustered.

Alex pushed another spoonful of vegetable medley to his lips. He was unimpressed.

"Well, I just came to say 'hi' real quick, and I'll go now, but I'll come back some time." I was lying. I wouldn't be back. I was going to call Verdugo Hospice as soon as I left and tell them to find someone else. It was bad enough burying people. But watching them die, too? No thanks.

I turned to leave, and to my surprise, Alex spoke.

"Stay! Pull up a chair!" he said, peas spilling out of his mouth. He made a wide motion to a folding chair in the corner.

I pulled it over and sat next to him. I knew from his paperwork that Alex was only 72, but the man in front of me looked 90.

"Who sent you?" he asked, eyeing me suspiciously.

"I'm a hospice volunteer. I'm just here to come by and make sure you're doing okay."

Alex clicked his tongue. "They don't care!" His voice boomed, despite his condition.

"Sure they do, and I do! How's your day?"

We stared at each other for a moment.

"Nice tits," he said, finally flashing a smile at me.

"Excuse me?"

"Nice teeths," he repeated, pointing to his mouth. I raised an eyebrow at him.

A wail came from the other side of the curtain.

"Shut up!" Alex said, then mumbled some Armenian. "This one, he cries all day, I can't stand."

There was a bulletin board above his bed. I stood up to have a look at it.

"Is this your family?" I asked.

"I have two daughters. But they don't come. They don't come if you don't have the money to leave them." He laughed, then pursed his lips.

I couldn't tell if he was joking or not. I turned away from his watery gaze, wondering how long it'd been since I'd spoken to my own father.

I visited Alex often.

"My angel," Alex bellowed as I entered his room, planting wet kisses on both of my cheeks. "This girl, she came to my life and change it," he said to the Filipino nurses flitting in and out of the room. "Have you met my girlfriend? My angel?"

They pushed his pills at him and walked away like deaf mutes. For the people that didn't have anyone come to visit them, that was what they got: A stone-faced woman making minimum wage, propping them up, pushing a plate of peas and pills in their face. Age and impending death had made everyone the same here. The nurses didn't get attached and the barren walls made it so that no one had a story.

Sterile rooms housed slow decay. A faint smell of feces lingered. The woman in 202 could've have been an opera singer or a schoolmarm. The grey man shuffling down the halls with vacant eyes could've been a physician or an Army captain. My Alex came from a foreign country with nothing in his pockets and started a taxicab company. Now he was ignored by a minimum-wage staff.

What made families stop visiting their loved ones in places like this? Was it really like Alex said... if you didn't have money to leave, your family didn't bother? Or were they just scared, scared shitless of their own mortality after wasting their life away in a cubicle? Or maybe that woman in 202 had mentally abused her children and they were glad she was rotting. Did 113 diddle his grandkids?

I had been visiting Alex three days a week for two months. He liked it when I would share his dinner with him. He would divvy up his meager portions and watch me spoon it into my mouth. It was his way of taking care of me. While we ate, we'd talk about politics and culture. He was opinionated and fiery.

"I hate the Armenians from Armenia. I am Armenian from IRAN, we different! They are rude... they are not like Armenians should be," he would say, clicking his tongue. "All they care about is money, they drive around their fast cars."

Alex began to leave his bed for the first time in months and sit in the hallway outside of his room. He requested a folding table be brought out and placed in front of his wheel chair, and arranged papers and pens on it, like his very own makeshift office. From his spot, he surveyed the nursing home and cat-called the nurses.

He always knew when I was coming.

"My angel! I hear your shoes!" Alex clapped his hands together in excitement as my high-heeled cowboy boots staccatoed across the vinyl floor in sharp contrast to the nursing shoes of the staff.

"Alex! Are we going for a walk today?" I gave him a hug and kiss, and got behind his wheel chair.

"No, no, we don't have to! Let's sit here! I like it here," he said, making a tut-tut noise with his tongue.

"It's good for you," I said.

He tensed in his chair. As I wheeled him down the hall, he held his robe tightly around him, shielding himself from the rot surrounding him. Zombies walked down the hall past us with catatonic stares. If the nursing home was Alex's own private horror show, the cafeteria was its creepy cellar. He squirmed and clicked his tongue as I led him past his drooling peers that spoke gibberish and wore adult diapers. A woman sat in front of her untouched plate of food and glared at us.

"Hello, Mrs. Phillips," I said. No one ever came to see her.

I wheeled Alex back to his "office" and we sat in silence for a while, sharing his apple juice.

"Before you came to see me, I would hide all of my pills they gave me under my mattress," he finally said. "When I had enough, I took them all in one night. But I still woke up the next day! I can't believe this! I was going to start saving the pills again, but then you come, my angel."

The next time I visited Alex, he was sitting in a folding chair outside of his room, instead of his old wheelchair.

"My angel, I have a surprise for you!" He extended his hand to a nearby nurse, and stood slowly. Then, like an infant learning to walk, he swung one leg in front of the other until he had made it halfway down the hallway.

"Alex! When did this happen?"

"He wanted to impress you!" The nurse winked at me.

"I've been practicing for you," he said.

I hugged him close, his papery cheek against mine. I wrapped my fingers around his and squeezed. It was a familiar feeling, almost like déjà vu...

I realized that I had been doing this half of my life. Chester, Richard, Alex, they were all the same. They were all in search of some sort of human con‑ nection that could only be transferred hand to hand. They went to great lengths to find it in bars and din‑ gy motel rooms. Alex was *still* looking for it on his deathbed. Was I looking for it, too?

I wished I could go back to being eight years old, to a time and place I had tried so desperately to forget after all of these years. I wished that I could go back to the day that I had watched my father cry and refused to hold him. I wished I could go back to that place in my soul where I wasn't a stripper or a courtesan to a man's hotel room; I was just my father's daughter. I would hold his hand in mine. Maybe change the course of history. Sometimes what we need is right there in front of our face. It's right fucking there.

As we ate dinner together that evening, Alex was even more charming than usual. "Darling, I forgot to tell you about the nice place I got under a tree... You'll come visit me there, won't you?" he asked.

"Sounds fancy, Alex," I laughed at him.

"Get the papers from my room, I show you," he said.

I went into his room and grabbed a pamphlet off of his nightstand. It was for Forest Lawn. I had almost forgotten that he had to die.

30.

TELL ME WHAT I'M NOT, AND I'LL SHOW YOU WHAT I AM

THE MEAGER PAY AT THE MORTUARY still had me dancing at Sam's a few nights a week. And when he didn't feel like going to the ol' Hof Brau to see me, I still saw Richard at the Motel 6. We would eat our Subway sandwiches, watch an episode of "Family Guy" on TV, and then I would strip down to my underwear and dance for him. After dancing for a while, I would lie down next to him and he would hold me close, breathing in my hair, gurgling happy behind me. We'd had the same routine for nearly a decade.

One morning, I got an email from Richard that caught me by surprise:

Most beautiful, most special, most magnificent Autumn:
I have made a resolution to avoid you from now on. As you may have heard me mention (about a thousand times), I love you. I have been in love with you (or obsessed with you,

anyway) for many years, almost 10 (many marriages don't last that long). And while I love being with you, it is a source of intense frustration (higher highs and lower lows) when, after hanging out with you, I don't see you for a while, whatever the reason. I actually go through several days of withdrawal after seeing you, and that doesn't even begin to count sexual frustration.

As was pointed out to me last Friday night by the friendly "MILF" at bowling, there are women who genuinely enjoy being with me (without being paid), who actually want to be with me and have sex with me (she thinks you have made me socially inept; perhaps I always was). Having met you in a strip club, the nature of our "relationship" was cast forever, and it is not what I really want or need in my life. You are so very special and so extraordinarily beautiful, that I have been unable to make this decision for all these years, but now, with the help of some understanding and accommodating female friends, I am trying to break free of my rather unhealthy obsession and will do so. Maybe my brother's sudden and unexpected death was a wakeup call that life can be short and that I must live it to the fullest, so that's what I'm planning to do.

I will never be with you the way I want to be with you, so I must say goodbye.

No doubt I'll always love you; you'll always have a very special place in my heart that no one will be able to replace, but I must now, as they say in the movies, "move on."

I wish you happiness, love, success, and prosperity, and hope that some day, I'll read about you, the famous Autumn Franklin, in the papers.

Goodbye my love,
Richard

I didn't reply back. I had nothing to say. He was right, it was time for him to say goodbye. It was also time for me to move on. I looked at my duffel bag of dance clothes on the floor. I wrinkled my nose at the acrylic heel poking out of it.

Sometimes over morning coffee, I'd peruse Craigslist. I liked to laugh at the missed connections section, and marvel at the number of men with an affinity for posing with Coke cans next to their penises in the "men seeking women" category. Once in a while, I'd take a glance at the "musicians wanted" section, just for old time's sake.

One morning I saw an ad that piqued my interest. It was for a band that featured four girls that sang punk rock covers with black electrical tape X-ing out their nipples. They needed a fifth. I stared at the advertisement on my computer screen for a good long while. It had been a decade since I'd moved to Los Angeles with dreams of being part of a successful rock 'n' roll band. It had been 10 years since Mike had left me on my living room couch and called me a stupid kid. Eh. It was too long ago. My time had passed. I closed my computer screen.

The next morning I found myself thinking about the advertisement again. I logged back on to Craigslist and found it. I reread the words.

"I'm thinking of auditioning for this," I said to Dylan.

He peered over my shoulder. Dylan was finally out of art school and working long days at his new job.

"I don't know," he said.

"What do you mean?"

"I mean, why would you want to get your hopes up?"

My face reddened. Didn't he think I was good enough?

"I used to play in bands all the time," I said.

"But that was, like, high school, right? It's time to grow up, Autumn." He kissed me on top of the forehead and went to make his coffee. "I know you have this problem with growing up. That's why you still strip. But it's time to start thinking about it."

My chest was tightened. As soon as he left for work, I emailed the advertisement.

Two days later I met a smarmy-looking manager named Frank and his blonde assistant in the parking lot of a North Hollywood rehearsal studio. Frank looked me up and down with approval. I had passed the first test; I was hot. The assistant was jumpy. Her eyes darted about like a candidate for a meth recovery program as she led me to a corner studio where four girls and three boys skulked back at me. She pointed at each girl as she announced their names: Nora, Kelsey, Belinda, and Heather. Heather poked Kelsey and pointed at my fringed boots. They giggled. A lanky boy named after a city I'd never been to clutched his guitar, and a dreadlocked guy sat behind his drum kit.

I watched them rehearse for a few songs. The girls were in full show mode, tossing their hair back and forth, pumping tiny manicured fists. They flashed daunting looks at me every now and then, as if to say, *Fuck you, bitch, you'll never be one of us.* Or perhaps it was just my own fragile ego, trying to dissuade me. I was shaking by the time it was my turn to get up and sing The Misfit's "Where Eagles Dare"—a song their manager had insisted I learn. Heather awkwardly shoved her microphone in my hand. I hadn't sung into a microphone in a decade.

When the boys started playing the opening chords to the song, it sounded completely different than it had when I had sung it by myself in the car. Did I even learn the same song? Red faced, I began to croak out the first verse. Then to my surprise, my knees stopped shaking. The chorus came easy. I turned to Nora and shook my hair in her face as I entered the second verse. By the end of the song, I was on my knees in a pose fit for a punk rock queen. Or at least for a girl who was willing to put tape on her nipples and jump around in front of a crowd singing cover songs.

I said my goodbyes to the girls, and the manager and his blonde assistant walked me out.

"So... can you be ready by this Monday? We have a show at the Viper Room."

It was Thursday. I had three more days to learn the songs. My heart pounded. The Viper Room on Sunset Boulevard!

"I think so! I mean, yes. Yes, I can!"

"Okay, I'll get you a set list. You'll need to learn eight songs, and the girls will teach you the choreography over the weekend."

"Cool," I said, bursting on the inside.

I got in my car, drove away, and then pulled into a 7-11 parking lot where I screamed. I had a band! I was a part of something again! I was in a band! I drove home to tell Dylan.

When I opened the front door, he was drawing at his workbench. I watched him from a distance. He was a beautiful man with chiseled features. I had fallen in love with him quickly and truly believed that he, along with my corpses, had saved me from myself. He looked over at me and smiled.

"You look nice, where have you been?" he asked.

"I went to audition for that band." I looked down at the floor.

"The band on Craigslist? I thought we talked about that and you weren't going—"

"I have a show Monday at the Viper Room," I said, smiling ear to ear.

His face fell. His right eye twitched. It always twitched when he was irritated or nervous. He had perfect, full lips, and they turned white at the edges.

"Are you sure you want to do that?" he asked. "I seriously thought we were done with this entertainment business bullshit. Where has it gotten you?"

"What?" My knees felt like they were going to buckle. It occurred to me that he had been counting on me failing. He didn't even really know me, after all these years.

"Are you really sure you want to do that?" he repeated. "Shouldn't you be thinking about getting a full-time job?"

His words took me back to my childhood. When I was six years old, my grandmother took me to the Fischer Theatre in Downtown Detroit to see *Seven Brides for Seven Brothers*. The theater captivated me. Chandeliers dripped from the ceiling, bronze statues beckoned. It was the most beautiful place that I had ever seen; I would've been happy just walking the Fischer's halls for an afternoon. But then the show started! Men and women in costume leaped across the stage, singing and dancing. Back at home I talked about the show endlessly. I wanted to be a part of it so badly.

A few weeks later, my parents enrolled me in bal-let lessons. I lived for those lessons, and my leotards and tights and slippers. I was a roly-poly dervish while all the other girls in my class were tiny little birds, but that didn't stop me. I fantasized that I'd be the head ballerina in a big show. I'd have a painted face and I'd be thin and a man with prominent cheek-bones would throw me in the air, twirl me around. I would steal the show.

Ah, THE SHOW! A few weeks into ballet classes, our teacher announced that we were going to have a recital on a big stage in front of everyone's families. And we would wear fancy tutus! We had a routine to learn. I practiced in class, and then all night at home. Even lying in bed at night, I would practice my balle-rina positions. First, second, third, fourth, fifth. I was sure that when my parents saw me on stage in full costume dancing my heart out, they would see how wonderful I was. They would stop fighting, because they would be so excited about the prima ballerina that they didn't even know they had right under their nose. We would probably talk about New York, maybe even Julliard.

A week before the recital, we were supposed to bring money in for our costumes. Everyone else's parents brought white envelopes for the teacher, except my mother. My father had decided not to waste money on the tutu. I would not be a part of the show after all. That night, I watched him as he ate dinner. A new gold bracelet dangled from his wrist. At six, I had received my first lesson in selfishness. At six, I knew that if I wanted something, I would have to learn to get it for myself.

"Yes." I said. "Yes, I'm absolutely fucking sure I want to do this." I looked Dylan in the eyes, pushing my hair behind my ears as he stared back in disbelief. Then I turned around, went into the bathroom, and locked the door behind me, tears rolling down my face.

31.

PART OF SOMETHING

"O HHHHH MY GOD, DJ ASHBA IS MY favorite, too! He's so hot!" I gushed to Nora from the floor of her Hollywood apartment, as we compared notes on the hottest musicians we could think of. "But you don't fuck the hired help, and since I'm still going to marry Axl Rose one day, I'd have to snub him, man!"

Nora unleashed her throaty, two-pack-a-day laugh and gave me a squeeze. All of the girls in the band were congregated in her living room to teach me the choreography for Monday night's show: fist pump cues, backing vocals, when to pour blood on my chest during the show. Nora was immediately my favorite of the group. She was a cute, pot-smoking little brunette with a tiny potbelly and big green eyes. I thought about how it might feel to make out with her.

Kelsey, who sat to my left ignoring me, reminded me of Courtney Cox. That is, if Courtney Cox hadn't been discovered at that football game and had taken

up a job at the local titty bar instead. She had pene-
trating blue eyes that held a look of constant shock, as
if she was always waiting for the other shoe to drop...
and knock her ass out. At my audition for the band,
I knew I recognized her from somewhere, and then
it finally hit me: She was a stripper that I'd worked
with for two days at Jumbo's Clown Room years before. My presence at Jumbo's had been well received
by the customers, but by the girls that worked there...
not so much. Instead of sharing the rather dim spotlight there with me, she told the boss lady that I was
giving hand jobs in the lap dance booth.

Unwilling to put up with a ridiculous hazing period, I quit Jumbo's which was the move that landed
me at Sam's Hof Brau. I could still picture Kelsey in
her cheap mesh robe, chastising me as I packed my
dance bag up. She didn't seem to remember me now,
and I was okay with that.

The one girl that looked severely out of place was
Belinda. Belinda was brawny and square. She had
a pixie haircut that didn't help her situation, but I
supposed somewhere there was a hipster that would
fantasize about being pinned down under such a girl.
Heather was the bombshell of the bunch. She had the
tits of the group: D-cups that filled her tank top to
the brim with sex. Miss Heather was a blonde, for-
mer cheerleader with a penchance for party metal
that had recently been given a crash course in punk
music courtesy of Frank D'onofrio.

Heather and I didn't say much to each other.
There was a connection between us that still had yet

to be determined. I wasn't sure if we would become best friends or dire enemies, but one thing was certain... we'd have to match each other's tenacity. Side by side, we went over the set again and again, weaves circle spinning in all of their clip-in glory.

When Sunday rolled around, I realized that I'd been so consumed with my new project that I hadn't seen Alex in an entire week. He'd be worried and lonely. I needed to change that.

I was excited to tell Alex about the band. Stuck in his tiny room, he loved to hear my stories of the outside world. I made my way down the familiar hallway, but as I rounded the corner to Alex's room I stopped in my tracks. There he was at his makeshift desk in his favorite spot, but he was surrounded by people. He hadn't even heard my boots! I recognized the people from the pictures on his wall; they were his family. They had (finally) come to see him. Alex was beaming and animated, waving his arms around and laughing. Jealousy coursed through me. Why were they here? They didn't deserve him, they had abandoned him, and he was mine now! Alex still hadn't spotted me, so I ducked around the corner, back down the hallway and out to my car. Tears welled in my eyes. Alex had looked so happy. I wanted that, too. That's all I'd ever wanted, to just be fucking happy.

32.

STAGE LEGS

THE SUN LIT UP THE CONDO I SHARED with Dylan like any other Monday morning. *The sun has no idea*, I thought to myself, stretching out my legs. Today was MY day. The day I would hop on-stage and perform as part of a band again. A day I had waited for, for a decade. Outside, Silver Lake Boule-vard buzzed with honking cars and garbage trucks. Bianca jumped off the bed, shaking off warm sleep. I turned on my side and watched Dylan spiking his hair through the open bathroom door. Being a work-ing man with projects and responsibilities and dead-lines had turned my schoolboy into a grownup. His eyes were serious and rejected the frailty of his youth. He had big ideas and overnight his gait had begun to command authority.

"You're coming after work, right?" I asked, my head propped on my arm.

"To your show? I thought we'd go together?" He peered out of the bathroom at me.

"Well... I guess the girls have this thing where

they like to get ready together." I felt like a traitor as the words spilled out of my mouth.

"Serious? So I just... meet you there?" he asked. "That's weird."

"If you want me to tell them I have to meet them there, I will." I crossed my fingers under the sheets. I didn't want to have to explain to the girls that I couldn't get ready with them because I had to accompany my boyfriend to the show. They would think I was a sap... fucking pussy whipped.

"No. It's fine. I'll just bring a friend. Whatever." He didn't look at me as he put his jacket on. I knew he was hurt.

"Well... have a good day at work." I sat up and piled the sheets around me.

Dylan left the room but then came back in as an afterthought. He sat next to me silently for a moment before tousling my hair and kissing me on the forehead.

After I heard the front door close behind him, I buried my head under my sheets. I had hours until I needed to be up, but there was no way I could sleep. I ripped the sheets off the bed and touched my feet to ridges in the parquet floor. I had ten hours until show time, but was I ready?

I opened my closet and fished out prospective costumes. I didn't need much: fishnets, my tall, black vinyl boots, two belts armored in pyramid studs, my favorite lock necklaces on their heavy chains, and my pleather boy shorts... no... two pairs of pleather boy shorts, in case of mishaps. I'd stripped in those

pleather shorts for years; oh, the laps they'd seen! Tonight they'd be used for a slightly higher purpose.

I laid everything out carefully on the bed and
stared at it all. I put the CD Frank had given me of all
of our songs in my Bose stereo and turned it up full
blast. I picked up my coveted pink Mason Pearson
brush from off the floor where I'd thrown it the night
before, and, taking a rocker stance in front of my bedroom mirror, I feigned punk rock excellence into its
bristles. I pointed to an imaginary crowd and snarled.
Bianca, back in her respective spot on my bed, looked
up at me, blinking and unimpressed. She was right; I
probably looked ridiculous.

At seven o'clock, I met the girls at Kelsey's West
Hollywood apartment, which had the geographical
gold star of only being two blocks from the infamous
Viper Room. Years before, River Phoenix had over-
dosed in front of the Viper Room. Tonight, I'd be
playing it.

The girls had an easy camaraderie with one another. They teased each other and listened to music
while they painted their faces and X-ed their nipples
with electrical tape. There was an art to the nip-
ple-taping. Placement and size of the strip was key.
The tape couldn't be too long or too short. There had
to be four pieces on each side. It couldn't look too
perfect, either. I mean, this was punk rock, not Playboy. My hands shook as I attempted my first strips.
The pieces of tape curled under my fingers. Kelsey
rolled her eyes at me as I used more than my allotted
share of that black gold.

"I'll bring my own next week," I said apologetically. On my fourth or fifth try, and on boob number two, I finally got it right; one piece for a half a nipple, and the next saddled up, just slightly overlapping, the next two on top of those pieces, for a perfect X-ed out mammary. After I was properly taped up, I painted my eyes a sooty black and clipped in a row of pink hair extensions. I stood back and looked at myself in Kelsey's mirror. It was crusted over with hairspray and layers of makeup dust. She flitted in and out of the room behind me, turning in circles. Nora screeched from the hallway. It had been a long time since I had looked in a mirror and really liked what I saw. A 17-year-old version of myself getting ready for a show with my high school band winked back at me from the glass.

"Hello, I missed you!" she said, and was gone. I felt beautiful. I felt at peace and ready for the evening. Then... I had an overwhelming desire to shit. *Now, really?* I didn't even know these people. My stomach cramped. There was one piece of toilet paper left on Kelsey's roll. I'd have to ask for more. Clutching my stomach, I went to the living room.

"Kelsey! Do you have more TP?"

"It's the nervous shits... we all get them," Heather said, smirking.

I wondered if she'd put Visine in my water bottle.

Like some rock gang initiation, I took a dump in Kelsey's bathroom and we were off.

The Viper Room was already full when we made our entrance. We shuffled into a tiny backstage room and picked at our fishnets until it was almost time to go on.

"Berenjager?" Kelsey offered me a pull off of a paper bag. I gladly accepted. I thought I'd completely unleashed the contents of my stomach in her bathroom, but my stomach gurgled like a fresh cup of Alka-Seltzer. Heather farted next to me, low and loud, and giggled. Maybe she hadn't poisoned me after all. I laughed with her, as the boys in the band drinking their Jack covered their noses in offense. Despite the lightened mood, I'd never been more nervous in my life. I thought about turning around and walking out the door. I wanted Dylan. I wanted our life back, the easy life where it was him and I, and I loved him and didn't need or want anything more. What had happened to that?

I closed my eyes and remembered us on a bed in a hotel room in Seattle many, many moons ago, looking into his brown eyes flecked with yellow and knowing that he was mine and I... I was his. Maybe he'd been right about all of this. I shouldn't have gotten my hopes up. Maybe my time was over. I shouldn't have bothered.

"Five minutes!" Frank hollered through the backstage door.

Or maybe... maybe that had never been real, and this was it. Maybe I had been waiting in a half slumber for way too long. I had become complacent.

"Ole, ole, ole, ole..." the girls erupted in a chant usually reserved for soccer games. Turns out it was the perfect warm-up exercise for girls that were about to screech out Black Flag cover songs live and in the flesh.

I joined. "OLE, OLE, OLE!"

It was almost like a war cry to myself. I was battle-ready as Frank pulled black cloaks over our heads—our tatas wouldn't be on full display until we actually hit the stage; they were shrouded in mystery for our walk. The Viper Room's sound system blasted out an intro to our set, a haunting voice foretold of wicked women as we navigated through the crowd and up the stairs to the tiny stage. When the voice ceased, the boys ripped into the Misfits and we dropped our hoods. The fear dropped from my body immediately along with the cape. We banged our heads relentlessly while the crowd leered and lunged like pubescent boys.

By the third song of the night, my solo song, I'd found my stage legs. I grabbed my microphone, elbows widespread, channeling my inner Glenn Danzig and ripped into "Where Eagles Dare." As I sang, I looked at Dylan in the crowd. He'd been my safety net for the last few years, and would also be so now. He nodded at me from the crowd and smiled slightly. For a moment, it was just us two. Then his cheeks blanched and his eyes turned glassy and I knew he was seeing a completely different girl than the one that rested her head on his shoulder in his Cadillac. I had needed to be his girl, *that girl*, for a while. I was convinced that, in some ways, being that girl had kept me alive. But it had saved me in the way that someone rescues a bird with a broken wing. You fix it, then you let it go again, because you know that the bird needs to fly. And they never come back. They never do. Fuck what the fairy tales say.

"You were good tonight, Autumn," Dylan said when I rejoined him in the crowd. "Real good."

33.

LOVE IS SUFFOCATING

SUDDENLY A MOTORCYCLE WAS BEING built in the spare room on the weekends. Newspaper lay beneath it, tools around it, and boxes of ordered parts were brought by the UPS man twice a week. A table saw had been abandoned in our living room and there were bathroom tiles that required completion, as well as a kitchen that needed remodeling in our fixer-upper condominium, but the little Café Racer that dripped oil in my spare room held precedence over all of these things. Dylan had become obsessed with it. As soon as he came home from work he would check in on it, as if I'd mussed it during the day. The weekends were exclusively for him and his newfound passion.

Before I woke up on Saturdays, he'd be off on a two-hour joyride through the hills. At night, he would go to Café Racer clubs and drink beers with his newfound friends that I had yet to meet. When I got home from work I would watch him as he slept. Half of me wanted to throw my arms around him and rub my face in his sandy hair. The other half of me wanted to smother him with a pillow. It was better to lie stiffly on my side of the bed. I felt abandoned all over again.

My band kept me busy. We had rehearsals two times a week and residencies at the Viper Room and the Roxy Theatre on Sunset. I was enjoying being part of the scene again, part of SOMETHING again. Dylan was not so fond of my deep interest in the band, and it continued to dig a wormhole between us. It was as if our chemical attraction had been fueled by his parent's fury. And like a 16-year-old who eventually gets bored with dry humping in a backseat, we did too.

Dylan had been acting funny for a week when I saw him packing an overnight bag. "What're you doing?" I asked.

"I'm thinking about going on a motorcycle camping trip after work. Just overnight," he said.

"Well, were you going to tell me?"

"I didn't want you to get mad." He avoided my gaze as he spoke.

"So it'd be better to just go? Why would you do that?"

"Autumn, I don't want to fight about it, don't yell at me!"

I seethed under my skin. How was he turning not telling me into my fault?

"Why couldn't you tell me earlier in the week?"

"I just didn't want to fight! God!" Dylan threw his bag over his shoulder, looked me in the eyes, closed the door, and left. I knew that he wouldn't be home the next day either. I looked at the table saw and the upside-down motorcycle in the study. I felt like I was suffocating.

Finality comes in a quick wave sometimes. Dylan came home after two days in the mountains with the boys and began to pack. We both knew it was over. I looked at him from a distance as he went through his things. He was as handsome as the first day that I had ever seen him. When we used to drive around in his Cadillac and I'd look over at him in his polo shirt, I'd want to pinch myself, I'd felt so lucky. I wanted to stand in front of him, unpack his things and tell him that I couldn't manage without him.

Before he left, he grabbed me by the shoulders. "The girl I fell in love with was going to mortuary school and wanted to be an embalmer. All this other stuff is too much for me. I'm sorry."

I closed my eyes, taking in the weight of his hands on my shoulder.

Motorcycle crash. That's how he went. He knew I never had a thing for his motorcycles. In the emergency room they'd tried to save him but he was dead on arrival. Brain swelling. A head skidding across the pavement never turns out well. His body was shredded, torn apart from the gears and spokes and heavy machinery that had landed on top of him in the accident. I wanted to be the one to put him back together. It had to be me. I washed his body and his sandy brown hair, bits of matter running down the drain. I stitched his fingers back together— he'd always had such beautiful hands—and puttied over the stitches. I made it seamless. It had to be seamless. I filled the hole in the left side of his head with Plaster of Paris and cov-

ered it in soft wax and foundation. He was beautiful. I dressed him in a white t-shirt and his favorite motorcycle jacket. I lay next to him for a little while and held him one last time. He was a good boy, he was. His family flew down from Seattle for the funeral. His mother passed out when they lowered the casket. I threw one yellow rose on top of it. Goodbye my lover, goodbye my friend.

Bianca died a month after Dylan left. They'd always had a special relationship. I had been jealous of it—spiteful, even—that the dog I'd rescued favored him. I would come home from work to find them wrapped around each other in our bed. They were soulmates. They were connected.

She was limp in my arms when I drove to the veterinary office. I carried her in and they told me there was no hope. I begged them to put her on an I.V. I couldn't put her to sleep. I couldn't do it. She was all that I had. I sat with her for hours, fingering her velvety ear, while she stared back at me with her big blue eyes.

I only left for a moment. I needed some food. When I came back, she was gone. They didn't want me to see her. I screamed and begged until they led me down the hallway to where she lay in a cage. Green bile seeped out of her snout. I collapsed to the ground. I couldn't leave until the veterinarian's office was closing for the day, and the receptionist pulled me off the floor. I couldn't believe she had left me. I'd never felt more grief in my entire life.

34.

MY FATHER'S DAUGHTER

I HADN'T SEEN ALEX IN OVER A MONTH. I was riddled with guilt as I parallel parked my car next to the Glen Oaks nursing home. I briefly considered turning around and heading home. I felt as much apprehension as I had the first day that I'd opened those glass double doors, in search of room 163. *Maybe it was better to just let him forget about me completely,* I thought to myself; let him think his angel never existed.

I walked down the hall to his room, my heels making their familiar click clack on the laminate floor. Alex wasn't at his desk in his favorite spot in the hallway. My heart jumped in my chest. My feet froze. I didn't want to know, but I had to.

I swung his door open and there he was, a bag of bones in his bed, nearly as white as the linen draped haphazardly across him. I went over to his side, kissed his forehead, and reached down to wrap my arms around him. He turned his head and pursed his thick, dry lips.

"Who are you?" he asked, facing the wall.

"Alex, don't do that." He drew further away from my touch. "I'm sorry I've been so busy. You wouldn't believe how busy, actually..." My voice trailed off and I cleared my throat. What did he care about busy? He was trapped within these four pastel walls all day, all night, smelling his roommate's bedpan.

I grabbed his hand and stroked it until he turned around and looked at me.

"I am so sorry I haven't been here, Alex."

"I missed you, my angel." Bits of skin flaked from his mouth as he talked.

"I missed you, too," I said. And then I burst into tears. I couldn't tell him that I had seen his family and hated them. I couldn't tell him that it had made me pull away. I could barely admit it to myself. "I abandoned you! I'm sorry. You needed me and I didn't come because I was too busy being selfish."

"Darling, shh shh shh!" Alex shushed me in Armenian. "What's the matter? Why are you crying? Why are you not yourself?"

And that was just it. I was not myself. I had been so wrapped in finally finding some peace with another human being that I'd forgotten who I was. I was Autumn Franklin. I had come all the way to Hollywood with a purpose a decade before. I was almost there.

I looked up at Alex's wall and noticed that he had new pictures of his family up.

"Your family is one thing you always have, no matter what. If you have family, you have everything.

If you have love, you have everything," he said, noticing my interest in the photographs.

"But I thought you said before that—"

"Sometimes an old man can be wrong." Alex pinched my cheek. I sat next to his bed and listened to the news with him on his radio until he started to snore. I kissed his forehead and tiptoed out the door. It was the last time I would ever see him alive.

Back at home, I sat in the solitude of my condominium. I decided to do something that I hadn't done in a very long time. I picked up the phone and called my father.

"Hello?" His voice sounded just like it always had.

"Hi Dad, it's Autumn." I tried not to cry. He hated weakness. Or was it me that hated weakness. "What're you up to?"

"Just watchin' the game, what about you?" There were always long pauses before my father spoke. We never really knew what to say to each other. I tried not to call unless I had something life changing to say.

"Oh nothing, just my band," I said.

"Yeah... I saw y'all singing on the internet with tape on your titties. Don't quit your day job!" He chuckled at his own joke.

"I'm pretty proud of it, actually. People love us."

"Mmmhmmm." He cleared his throat. "Well, I saw some interview you did about Detroit. It kind of made me mad. You said how it was hard for you growing up. It wasn't that bad."

"Actually, it was." I paused and took a deep

breath. "It was, Dad. You weren't around that much, so you might not know. But it was hard. Really hard." I wanted to reach through the phone and shake him. Make him wake up and realize what he'd missed.

"Well, I wish I would've known that."

"I guess I could've called you and told you." My voice quivered. "I gotta go. Just wanted to say hello."

"Well, I love you."

"I love you, Dad."

Once, when I was out to dinner with my father, brother, and Grandmother Renata, I asked my dad why he had given away all of our pets when we were little kids. One after another, they would disappear, leaving us heartbroken. My father's expression had turned almost childlike after my accusation, and he pointed across the table at Grandmother Renata.

"Well, she gave away my dog when Denise was born!" he said. The garlic cheese roll in my grandmother's hand fell to her plate. I learned more about my father in that instant than I did knowing him for a lifetime. It suddenly occurred to me that often times those who aren't the easiest to love are the ones who probably need it the most. I was truly my father's daughter.

35.

REBIRTH

Highland Park, California, 2012

ANTHONY CAME OUT TO THE FRONT OF the duplex to collect me off the curb. He sat down beside me, his long legs dangling off the steps.

"What's the matter? You don't like it?"

"No, I love it. I'm just overwhelmed." I looked up at him. I had told him the first lie I would ever tell him. I wasn't overwhelmed. Not in the least. For the first time in my life I knew I wanted this more than anything. What I was... was afraid. I was used to fighting. Struggling. Being angry. How would it feel to just be okay?

I pushed my way through the crowd into the dressing room at Sam's Hof Brau later that night, secured a prime spot for my dance bag, and started undressing. All around me, girls clamored to get ready for the night shift. They glued on fake eyelashes, teased their hair with rat combs, hid their stretch marks with Sally Hansen leg spray, and doused themselves with drugstore perfumes. Strippers alone had made cotton candy body spray a million-dollar industry.

The girl next to me arched her back towards the mirror. "Girl, I want a stupid booty," she said, holding her dimpled ass in her hands. "This lady in El Monte will give you a stupid booty for, like, two G's."

I smiled at her, stepping into my acrylics. Why couldn't they make regular shoes as comfy as acrylic stripper shoes? No Christian Louboutin's on the planet could feel as easy as these shoes, wrapped around my tattooed feet with strips of industrial plastic.

It was a busy night. As soon as I walked out onto the floor, a customer grabbed my arm and led me back to the lap dance area. I sat on him and started to grind.

"Can you do it harder? I like it harder!" His cock bulged under his thin linen pants. "And stick your ass out more, like this," he said, shoving my lower back down with the palm of his hand.

When I was tired of squatting, I turned around and rubbed my thigh against his cock as I looked at myself in the mirror behind the lap dance booth. I was remarkably well preserved. I didn't look much different than I did at twenty-one. I still weighed exactly one hundred and nineteen pounds, my ass was still firm. My tits, god bless Dr. Linder, were aesthetically-pleasing, high beam 34 C's. I'd always had pesky hereditary dark circles under my eyes that I slathered with hundred dollar eye creams and concealer, but not a crow's foot in sight. I had grown to live with the dog bite scar on my cheek, the laugh lines I'd had since I was a kid, and the stretch marks that had been with me since puberty made my hips, ass, and thighs swell into their current stripperific proportions.

I had given up the late night Taco Bell runs and cocaine, and spent a healthy hour and a half at the gym every day. Most customers guessed my age to be around 24. I've been telling the same schmucks 26 for years now. Only a select, persistent few knew the truth. Point being, I potentially had many good years of peeling left in me. But I had many years behind me, and my goal never was to become a lifer. The aging Asian flower with 10 boob jobs under her belt; the 50-year-old Pamela Anderson wannabe with cheek implants distorting her leathery face, stringy make-shift extensions hiding the scar of the wreckage of her own existence. I'd spent enough time in this life raft.

I turned away from his gaze, sitting back down on his cock.

"Seriously, you can do it harder... that's what I like. And put your legs like this," my customer said, putting his hands on my thighs. His fat fingers left red welts in my skin. *Enough time in the life raft.* I bent back his fingers and stood up. I turned around and looked at him. He squirmed in his seat, cock throbbing under his pants.

"You're a filthy piece of shit," I said to him.

"Hey! At least I don't show my tits for a dollar!" he retorted, licking his lips. Well, he had a fucking point there. I looked him in the eye. I thought about all the things that I could do to him. I could slap him.

Or slam his head into the mirrored wall behind him. I could take the beer bottle that sat on the table next to me and bash it against his skull. I could gouge his eyeballs out with the broken end of said beer bottle. He just simply wasn't worth it. None of it was worth it anymore. I walked away without asking for my pay.

"Bitch!" he called after me.

I walked back to the dressing room. Cathartically, I took off my bikini and put it back into my dance bag. I put my acrylic pumps away. I re-dressed in my street clothes and threw my bag over my shoulder.

"Leaving already? You were barely out there, girl, go get you some money!" Annette, the house mom, called after me as I walked out the door. I walked back through the crowd, pausing in the middle of the room to look at my reflection one last time in long mirrored wall in front of me.

And that's the moment I killed her. I knew that it had to be done, and I had to be the one to do it. I put a gun in her mouth. The taste of metal made her gag a little. I almost chickened out. I closed my eyes, pulled the trigger, and blew her brains against the wall. The blood spattered on the customers and stained their shirts. They didn't even notice. They kept drinking their beers, even after she had bled all over them. I watched her struggle for a moment with the situation; she put her hand to the hole in her head and tears welled in her eyes. She looked back at me accusingly. I saw her at five with her showgirl doll, at 18 with her long brown fall, in her 20s with her blonde curls. She reached for me once, as I turned to walk out the door. But she didn't cry out, she didn't try to stop me. She knew it was over. There'd be no retirement party, no fanfare, no long goodbyes, no ticker tape parade. There would be a small funeral. Her parents. Her lover. Past lovers. There would be white roses and she'd be buried in her motorcycle boots with the ashes of her dead dog.

Someone once said that death is a stripping away of all that is not you. The secret of life is to die before you die, and find that there is no death.

Anthony was in the kitchen making himself dinner when I got home.

"Hey," he smiled at me, and kissed me on the head. "That was fast... are you okay?"

I unzipped his hoodie and wrapped my arms around him underneath the soft fleece, burying my nose in his chest.

We were in New Orleans once and he picked out a charm for me from a vendor at a music festival. The charm was pearl white and smooth on one side, brown and rough on the other side. I overheard him say to the jeweler that it was perfect for me, because I had a certain duplicity about me. I knew when I heard him say that that he understood me better than anyone ever had. I knew that he saw me for who I truly was and loved me in spite of it.

"I'm happy," I said.

"My baby... you are the most beautiful thing I have ever seen," he said. His eyes were wet with love. You know the look. It only happens when it's genuine.

"I want to get that house for you," he said.

For the first time in my life, I believed in someone. Myself.

Printed in Great Britain
by Amazon